Bringing Up Mommy

The Tender Years

Bringing Up Mommy

The Tender Years

by

Debra-Lynn B. Hook

The (Columbia, S.C.) State

ANDREWS and McMEEL
A Universal Press Syndicate Company
Kansas City

Additional copies of this book may be ordered by calling (800) 642-6480.

Library of Congress Cataloging-in-Publication Data

Hook, Debra-Lynn B.
    Bringing up mommy; the tender years/by Debra-Lynn B. Hook.
        p.   cm.
    Includes bibliographical references.
    ISBN 0-8362-7035-5
    1. Motherhood—United States.   2. Child rearing—United States.
    3. Mothers—United States. I. Title
    HQ759.H74 1994
    649'.1—dc20   94-23848

                                                                    CIP

Dedicated to Steve,
Christopher and Emily.
May they always come first.

And to my mother and my late father.
Now I know.

Contents

Acknowledgments

This book would not have been possible without the support and prodding of loving friends and supportive colleagues, especially Claudia Smith Brinson and Jennifer Nicholson Graham, whose personal support and professional advice during the last seven years and particularly during final editing have been like a beacon in the dark. I am grateful to various other former and current colleagues at *The* Columbia, S.C. *State*, where *Bringing Up Mommy* was born, especially my editors, Fran Zupan and Megan Sexton, also Jim Foster, Betty Lynn Compton, Dargan Richards, Tom McLean, Gil Thelen, Frank McComas, Linda Waltz and various members of the photo staff, including Anne McQuary and Linda Stelter and especially Ginger Pinson, who took the first pictures of my first baby when he was 24 hours old. I wish to remember my former desk mate, Michael Lewis, wherever he is, for encouraging me to write my first column, and fellow author B.J. Ellis, who introduced me to the writings of Anna Quindlen and helped brainstorm the title of this book. Thanks go to Karen Kirk of Knight-Ridder Tribune News Service and to Jake Morrissey and Regan Brown of Andrews and McMeel, all of whom have supported this project with unending patience. I wish to thank Professor Mac H. Brown at the University of South Carolina for sharing his expertise on early childhood development. I wish most especially to acknowledge the many friends who have given me the support and wisdom I needed to continue chronicling my personal life these many years, including Deborah Hazlett and Jeff Miller, Kelly Gosnell and Mike Dickert, Dr. Judy Sullivan, Margaret Perkins, Dorothy Kahaly, Holly Gatling, Mary Williams, Anne Marie Rossi, my "Cakes" friends, my family in New Orleans and Los Angeles, and each and every reader who wrote, called or stopped me at the mall. I would like to thank my mentor and friend, Lynda Tassie, who allowed herself and her two children to be on the record for seven years, and counting. I would like to acknowledge a fifth member of our family, our children's first baby sitter, M.E. Perkins, who, through the purity of her friendship, taught me the meaning of true support and encouragement. My deepest gratitude goes, as always, to my husband, Steve, who graciously tolerated his frequent appearances in my columns and who pushed me relentlessly to pursue this book. Finally, I salute my children, Christopher and Emily. Their presence in my life is a constant source of inspiration. *Bringing Up Mommy* belongs to them.

Preface

*U*nlike my peers, I wasn't much of a baby sitter when I was a teenager. About the only experience I had with babies was when my sisters came home from the hospital and my mother told me not to touch them.

In fact, I never gave much thought to babies at all until, at 31, I found myself pregnant with one.

By most standards, this was not good timing. My husband had just started graduate school, and I was helping maintain the family by working full time as a newspaper reporter. We drove used cars and lived in a drafty rental house that measured 850 square feet, if you counted the back porch.

As it turns out, timing was nothing. From the moment the nurse at the family clinic confirmed my suspicions, I was smitten—the idea that I could grow a baby inside me! I loved announcing to family members around the country that I was pregnant. I loved "showing" for all the world to see. I even savored labor and delivery. And then there was the outcome. I can still remember how overcome I felt, holding my son for the first time and then my daughter.

Little did I know that having children would captivate me so. But they did. They have. And it's not just them and their fat little fingers and toes.

We are living in a time when parents are being forced to rethink the rules on family life. Women work outside the home in record numbers. Yet they continue to have an urge to bear and raise children. Women stay home with their children. But they aren't as revered as their predecessors. Communities aren't much help either. Extended families have disappeared. Neighborhoods have retreated inside. The how-tos of modern-day parenting are confusing to all of us, who used to step over the fence and ask the opinion of the woman next door.

The simple joys and complex trials of motherhood, children, family—all of it very quickly became my passion, and not just in the home where Barney, pizza stains and Legos prevail, but under the point of my pen.

Beginning with my fourth month of pregnancy and continuing into my son's seventh year of life and my daughter's third, I have had the profound opportunity of chronicling modern-day life with children in my "Bringing Up Mommy" newspaper column. My column has given me a place to test my emotions and to grow, not only as a mother struggling to find her way, but as a journalist; I ultimately found such fodder in the modern-day family that I shifted my writer's attention away from county council meetings and ribbon-cutting ceremonies to covering the child-care industry, parenting trends and family life in general. Today, I am no longer at the newspaper, having quit my full-time job two years ago so I could spend more time with the very children

I write about. But I continue to write from home about family, both in my column that runs twice a month in newspapers around the country and as a consultant for organizations committed to early childhood development and child care.

What started out as bad timing has become my life's work.

Motherhood has given me my writer's voice and something much more significant—the privilege of watching two sunflowers up close as they lift their faces to the sun.

I muse much about child care, the loss of the extended family and the politics of motherhood.

But the starting and ending point of this book is a mother's heart.

When all is said and done—when the baths have been given and the paper and pen put away—it is their round eyes and soft faces, it is my young children's hearts and voices that keep me putting one foot in front of the other. It is their resilience and trust, their hopeful outlook, their startling capacity for love.

Perhaps it's all about love—not that my little sunflowers are always so good at letting me smother them with kisses. But how lucky I am that they still seem to love me at the end of the day.

Debra-Lynn B. Hook
March 1995

Maternity clothes

May 2, 1988

*T*here comes a time in the life of every pregnant woman when she realizes she can't hold out any more.

She must enter the world of maternity fashion.

My time came Month 4, Day 10. That morning, I tried a trick that expands normal-sized clothes when you're slightly abnormal but don't need maternity clothes yet:

You simply insert a rubber band into the top button hole. Then you pull one end of the rubber band through the other, loop that first end around the button. Presto: an elastic waist band.

This worked for a few hours, but as the morning wore on, the rubber band became stretched to an unnatural length.

My discomfort was not helped by comments from a colleague:

"I bet you'd look pregnant if you wore real maternity clothes," she said.

"What do I look like now?" I asked.

"Like you've gained weight."

That was my cue. I would head for Maternity Outlet Wonderland at lunch.

At that moment, I was a little manic.

For one thing, I had just been given carte blanche to buy a new wardrobe.

Maybe if I looked pregnant I would finally believe that I was.

Perhaps I was most excited because after all these years I was finally going to look sweet and innocent again.

That is part of the allure of pregnancy—wearing flowing dresses of polished cotton and lace and standing in a field of daisies, your hands lightly touching your belly as you gaze into the distance.

But then you daydream a lot when you're pregnant.

The reality of semi-affordable maternity fashion, I discovered during my hurried lunchtime excursion, is poly/cotton pants with polyester stomach panels and cheap dresses with strings hanging off the hems. Even if I liked these clothes, I couldn't afford more than one and a half outfits, hardly enough to last until my water broke.

I wasn't any more encouraged at the department store downtown. The clerk told me after I found a parking place and huffed and puffed four blocks over and two stories up that they didn't stock maternity clothes.

"Why don't you try the large women's department?" she said, to the obvious glee of two young bikini shoppers who turned and smiled.

I wasn't about to go skulking around racks of clothes I'd struggled all my life to avoid. My lunch hour was gone anyway. And I had to face facts.

Not only was I going to wear this stupid, gnawing rubber band back to the office, but I had been duped by yet another set of feminine myths. Polished cotton, indeed. Sweet and innocent, ha. Maternity fashion is like bodies. You long to have the best, but it costs too much money.

Trudging up the steps of the newspaper with my skirt continuing to grind away at my waistline, I didn't feel pregnant. I felt defeated, like I do after the Christmas holidays when a tight waistband reminds me for two weeks that I ate too much pecan pie. And if pregnancy was this bad now, what was it going to be like two months from now, four months from now when I was resigned to wearing the tent dresses my mother used to wear when she was in a cleaning mood?

But then something changed my perception on life. Just that fast. Sort of like making a baby.

It was another woman. She phoned to say she'd heard I was pregnant. She wondered if I needed anything. Maternity clothes, maybe? She had a closet full she'd love to loan out. She could bring them to the office that afternoon. Oh, and they were designer maternity clothes. Would that be all right?

Would that be all right?

Pregnancy, coupled with poverty, removes all pride. From that moment forward, word began to leak out that the pregnant woman in the corner of the newsroom would even take recycled maternity underwear. One by one, women who were more than happy to forget thighs rubbing together and One Size Fits All came forward with billowing swimsuits, stretch pants and empire-waist dresses for the new kid on the block.

The next day was a joy.

I looked sweet, innocent and pregnant in my polished cotton designer maternity dress.

Pregnant, not fat.

This is really real. I am going to have a baby.

Something's moving.
It could be a baby.

May 23, 1988

A woman has to ask herself some pretty big questions when she finds out she's pregnant, to include: How is this going to affect my life? Do I stick with my gynecologist or find a midwife? Should my mother come now or later? Ever?

I look down at the growth that already hides my feet and continue to ask myself: Is there really a baby in there?

This must be a concern for all first-time pregnant women, one that doesn't begin to diminish until the third or fourth month, when she finally begins to show, to stick out enough that a stranger notices. It's a big moment the first time an outsider asks "When are you due, honey?"

Once past that milepost, begins the worried wait for "butterfly wings," which is what the books say the first fetal movements will feel like. This will help answer the question: Is the baby alive?

I was well into my fifth month before I felt anything other than excess gas. Then one weekend, my husband and I took a camping trip in the mountains. It was a quiet trip, mostly, although one morning we took a wild drive to the top of one of the mountains, loud music blaring out the car window. I ran around the peaks, laughing and jumping like I was 130 pounds and balanced.

I felt exhilarated as we drove down the mountain. But back on the main highway something strange and gurgly began to happen beneath my shirt. This was no butterfly. I could actually see a pocket of skin moving up and down over my rib cage.

Warnings from pregnancy books shot through my mind: Don't go into the mountains during the mid-to-later stages of pregnancy; thin air in higher elevations doesn't provide enough oxygen for the baby. Don't jump up and down. Stay away from loud music.

I put Steve's hand on my stomach. The look on his face didn't help, nor did his suggestion that we pull roadside and call a helicopter.

We instead ate lunch, which stopped the disturbance for a while. But the commotion returned several times that weekend, especially as I lay down to sleep on a tarp about a light year away from a doctor. Thump. Thump. Thump. Thump-da-thump. Thump-da-thump. Slurp. I had no choice but to put it out of my mind until we returned to civilization.

Thank goodness for civilization, especially a civilization that includes mothers who will happily talk all day about preserving the human species. My mother friends all looked at me with love and knowing in their eyes.

That was the baby, silly.

They proceeded to tell me more about fetal movement than I really needed to know, as mothers are wont to do, like how one woman's butterfly is another woman's alien. They told me some babies kick and others not at all. Some babies even keep beat with the music that eventually appeals to them, they claim.

I'm glad this activity has been labeled. Now I'm trying to determine whether we're going to have a rocker or a classicist.

That, and whether I'm carrying a human. It could be a watermelon. There's no way to be sure.

Where men dare not go

June 27, 1988

I kept gasping as my husband and I watched the ultrasound screen last week—partly because the doctor was pressing hard on my bladder—but mostly because there it was: Our baby.

There was the little head. There were the little hands balled up near the baby's face. There were the legs and the tiny feet. There was the heart, beating, and the spine, all in one piece.

My husband seemed suitably impressed. He said "Wow!" a lot. But then he left the doctor's office and went back to work.

I'm the one who can't forget.

Beyond catching a glimpse of a miracle on an ultrasound screen, I'm the one who gets to feel the foot tickling me from the inside. Sometimes the baby's little rear end will pop up on one side of my stomach. I get to take my hand and gently push it back down. And then the other side will pop up in defiance.

I'm reminded throughout the day in other ways. I can't stand for more than an hour, or my back hurts. I'm too tired to stay up late anymore, but then I can't get comfortable once I go to bed. Pregnancy is out there for everybody to see, so that daily, at least one person asks when I'm due, how I'm feeling, whether the summer heat is bothering me.

It's these constant reminders that have sent me into something akin to the Twilight Zone, only not nearly so foreboding.

I have put down the nuts and bolts, how-to-mommy books and picked up Nancy Caldwell Sorel's *Ever Since Eve*, a book of personal reflections on childbirth.

I don't wonder much any more about what the baby will be when he/she grows up, whether we'll let him/her date at 15 or 16, what we will do when he/she comes asking for the keys to the car.

I think these days about immortality, re-creation, rebirth—things of the spirit.

These are the things I talk about.

When I relay these thoughts to Steve, he listens. He smiles. Then he jokes, "You OK, honey?" And he goes back to sleep.

A woman wants to share as deeply as she can these moments, among the most magical that life has to offer. She especially wants to share with the man who helped her create the very thing that has enchanted her so.

And so she invites, sometimes drags, him to the ultrasound screenings. She picks up his hand and places it on her tummy so that he occasionally will feel when the baby gives a great, strong kick. She shares with him her

thoughts, trying desperately to explain what it's like to have a flower growing inside her body.

But no matter how hard either of them tries, this is one ride the male
species can't take all the way to the top.

I'm sure my husband must be relieved; the grand scheme of things
chose me and not him. He must be glad that I'm the one who tosses and
turns at night and needs a bathroom three times during a 90-minute drive to
visit my grandmother.

But doesn't he also wish for a minute?

Wouldn't he like to know?

I squirm. I complain. I wait.

Sept. 12, 1988

September 1.

And I was sure I wouldn't make it through the night without having a baby.

I was fidgety and mean, even more than usual, even for a woman who has
gained 43 pounds in eight months. I had bands of pain across my abdomen.
And I was craving and devouring chocolate—a sure sign, a grandmother
told me, that my body was storing up energy for labor.

For hours into the night, I sat alone on the couch in the living room. I
squirmed. I complained. I waited. Then I fell asleep.

That was 11 days and 11 nights ago. There have been many more "This
must be it!" nights.

I'm always so sure. And always: nothing.

If only we knew exactly when and how this life-rattling event will occur.

People could throw parties for us. We could stand at the mirror during
those last hours, properly grieving the impending loss of this unique relationship between mother and child.

We could plan. Knowing exactly how much time we had, we could time
the finishing of the nursery, the preparation of those vats of spaghetti we're
supposed to cook and freeze before the baby comes.

We could attempt to relax.

As it is, many of us can only estimate the moment of conception and/or
the dates of our last menstrual cycle, which leaves one of the great moments
of life a guessing game.

This is made more nerve-wracking by the myth of the Due Date, which
the physician pronounces with great surety throughout the pregnancy. He
pronounces. We cling.

"The baby will come September 29," my doctor first said with an imperious smile and a spin of the great gestation wheel.

Sometime in the middle of the pregnancy, a sonogram noted that the baby's head was bigger than it should be for a Sept. 29 baby.

"The baby will come in mid-September," the doctor said.

There was another ultrasound test.

"The baby will come any time in September."

Then recently, for no reason that I can ascertain, the doctor reverted with great finality to: "Late September. The baby will be born in late September."

It's no wonder we cling to the slightest flutter in our bellies, convinced that our babies are going to come *sooner* than anybody predicted. (Funny how we never predict *later*.)

I have suggested to the mothers who have gone before me that perhaps I have some control over this. Maybe if I jump up and down a lot, that will hurry the baby along. Maybe willing the baby out will make it come sooner.

Nah.

"Babies come when they want to," so they say.

Well, OK, little baby of mine, if you're concerned about life on the outside, let me tell you that I still haven't put any spaghetti in the freezer. Your dresser hasn't been sanded or stained yet.

But your bed is made. The Pampers are in the changing table. And I can't wait to see you.

I wish you'd come on out.

Only a mother can do this

Feb. 20, 1989

During pregnancy, a woman reads a lot of books and talks to a lot of mothers as she searches for answers to the questions: How will I know when it's time for the baby to come? What will I feel? She clings to mothers who had good birth experiences, hoping hers will be like theirs.

But as author and childbirth educator Fritzi Kallop says in her *Birth Book*, "As inconvenient as it is to have labor begin spontaneously, it seems fitting to have inexplicable forces controlling one of the most important events in life.

"Scientists may marvel as they observe the wonders of our farflung universe; it is equally miraculous to contemplate the birth of a child. Not one is ever routine."

And at some point, the mommy hopeful realizes there aren't any answers. Her experience won't be the same as anyone else's. It's hers alone to endure.

I began feeling the intensity of this predicament two weeks before my baby was due. Big and tired, I had decided to take maternity leave from work to rest up for the days and weeks ahead.

I thought I'd enjoy this time, sitting at home with my feet up and day-dreaming about holding my baby for the first time.

But at least at work, I could try to be like everybody else. At home, I was isolated, trapped by Oprah, Beaver and a phone that rang incessantly as people demanded to know, "Anything yet?" In the afternoons, the world bicycled and jogged past my living room window while I could barely pull myself off the couch to get a drink of water.

Finally, on the morning of Sept. 28, while I toddled alone about the confines of my house, I felt a trickle of water roll down my leg.

The nurse at my OB's office affirmed what I knew to be true: "It's time," she said.

I was excited as I arrived at the hospital. My husband and I settled into one of those *House and Garden* delivery rooms that makes you think you're going to have a cocktail party instead of a baby. Time settled into a warp as we lounged toe-to-toe on a mauve sofa under dim lights. We chatted intimately as contraction after contraction passed without a grimace. Perfect. We could have made a movie for Lamaze class.

But, oh, lest a laboring woman get too comfortable, the transition stage of labor, when the cervix opens that last little bit for the baby to emerge, was only gaining steam. Some women told me they moved up to this "real work" of labor gradually. For me, transition came fast. Nothing in the books, nothing that the mothers had said, could have prepared me for the intensity—or for the aloneness I felt.

I remember thinking I was the only one who could do this. I remember wishing I hadn't said I didn't want an epidural. I remember getting up on all fours because the baby wasn't getting enough oxygen. I remember feeling scared. I remember forceps.

I especially remember my husband dropping his head to my shoulder and saying "Thank you, God," when we were told we had a healthy son.

Then he was gone. Because the cord had been around his chest, they whisked my baby into the nursery before I could count his toes, look into his eyes, nurse.

I didn't get to "bond." Steve didn't get to cut the cord. I didn't feel any of those miraculous feelings.

The experience I had anticipated for months was over, my baby was gone and so was my husband, who went to stand watch at the nursery window. And I was left with the clean-up nurses who mopped up my body and wheeled me into a room where I choked down half a dry turkey sandwich and made a few phone calls. My husband came in and out of the room. He said I still looked pregnant.

Time settled into a warp again until sometime after dark, when Steve poked his head inside the door and said I had a visitor. I grimaced, wondering who would be coming to see us now.

Steve opened the door wide. A nurse came in, pulling a tiny cart behind her. I cried out as my baby was laid in my arms while his father looked on.

There had been nothing in the books to prepare me for the feelings I had then, either.

I was not alone anymore.

Missing you

March 20, 1989

At lunchtime today, I called home to find out whether Christopher was up from his morning nap and ready for me to come home and feed him.

But the idea of food was not high on my baby's list, his sitter told me. He'd been busy accomplishing a first.

"He turned over this morning—all by himself!" Mary said cheerily.

I was thrilled for my baby. Of course I was thrilled.

But I was the one who witnessed all the other firsts.

I was the I who saw him that one morning, shaking his little balled-up fist near his face and then suddenly freezing, and with crossed eyes, staring, as he discovered his own God-given hand. I was the one who watched when he lifted his head for the first time like a turtle. I was the one who saw his face when he realized he could touch the crib gym above his head and make it move. It was Mommy, who, when Daddy said, "Look, honey, he's grabbing his toes!" knew he'd already done that the day before.

When I have just a second to snap back to the four months of maternity leave that have just ended, this is what I recall, a magical time full of first, magic moments that I was privileged to witness because I was there.

In reality, I know it wasn't so ideal. I remember feeling inadequate much of the time. I felt like a mother, all right. I was lucky to be one of those mothers who loved her baby from the moment I held him in my arms. But love does not a mommy make, I found out.

There were all kinds of lessons to be learned, and they come at you constantly in those early days—little lessons, like how to put a tight shirt on: sleeve, then head, then sleeve. There were big lessons, such as one cry means "I'm tired" and another means "I'm hungry," and you'd better know the difference.

I often cried, myself, during those four months, as I reinvented new solutions to age-old complications like my breast infections and his confused nap schedules.

Yet despite the stresses of new motherhood, those four months went by so quickly. Now, the struggles seem far away. Now, all I readily recall are the magic moments.

I know I'm luckier than many. I got to stay with Christopher for four months, unlike many mothers whose job benefits, if they have any at all, force them back to work when their babies are six weeks old.

I'm lucky that Christopher's sitter is a wonderfully wise friend who loves my baby with all her heart. And he loves being with her. I live six minutes from work, and thus I'm able to go to him on my lunch hour. I'm lucky because my boss is the mother of two, and she understands.

But we bring these babies into the world so we can watch them grow and maybe learn something from them along the way.

And then what do we do?

We miss the firsts. We miss them.

I miss him so much.

The ear infection

June 19, 1989

I don't care how confident or sensible you think you are as a parent, when your baby gets sick for the first time, everything goes out the window.

I used to be confident. Sensible, too. It was easy. During eight months of life, my baby had had only two minor colds and a short-lived ear infection that cleared up with a mild antibiotic. Well-baby checkups always found my baby well. There were no allergies, no funny rashes. I skipped the chapters on health in the baby books.

But as quickly as a baby wakes from an afternoon nap, that's how quickly confidence can crumble.

Christopher went down for a nap healthy. He woke up with drippy eyes. Drippy nose. Heat emanating from his body. Body language of a rag doll.

From there, it could be any new parent's story:

"Oh, God," you beseech, as you dial the doctor with one hand and squirt Tylenol down the baby's throat with the other, "if only I hadn't turned the fan on him last night. If only I had covered him better when we were in the sun. If only I had thought to ask if any of the children at the church nursery were sick."

Of course, it's Sunday afternoon, and you have to go through the answering service to get the doctor. Of course, the doctor is swamped with calls and when he calls you back, he's in a hurry.

You're nervous, trying to register everything he's telling you to do, and by the time you hang up, you've forgotten how many teaspoonsful of Novahistine DX cough syrup—or was it Novahistine DMX?—he told you to give the baby.

Of course you don't have anything remotely close to what you think the doctor said you need, and your husband's not home to watch the baby, so you grab the baby and his favorite blanket and you run out the door to the nearest pharmacy.

And of course they don't have the right kind of cough syrup, and it's after 6 on a Sunday, and no pharmacists are working, and so you snatch the cough syrup you think might work. It's the one that has everything in it, expectorant, antihistamine and suppressant. On your way home, you realize you don't know what expectorant is, and so you stop at the pay phone, lugging the baby to the phone with you because you don't want him to be lonely in his misery, and you call the answering service.

You wait by the pay phone for the doctor to call you back and to tell you, yes, you're right; no, that's not the right cough syrup. "We don't want to knock him out," he says. (Don't we?) And the doctor tells you about another cough syrup you can get.

You go back to the pharmacy and look for the other cough syrup, which they also don't have. This time you grab the most innocent-looking one, the Bayer Children's in the pink box. You go to the customer service counter, you trade one cough syrup for the other, and you and baby go home.

Congratulations. You have just survived the first 30 minutes of your first baby's first illness.

But wait.

You still have the next day's visit to the doctor and the diagnosis to endure: dual ear infections in our baby's case.

There are the nights of not sleeping well: five for this mom, dad and baby, so far.

There are the droppersful of medicine to give: 19 a day, every one of them fought by a very strong baby.

There are the side effects of the medication: diarrhea, rash and irritability, in this case.

There are the bills from the pharmacy and the physician: $112 for us.

There is the creeping knowledge that this is just the beginning. There will be more ear infections and colds; measles, maybe; chicken pox, undoubtedly; throw-ups on the carpet; skinned knees and a broken arm or two.

There will be that overwhelming helplessness for you to endure every time.

But then one day, your baby laughs. Or he smiles when you kiss his toes.

He reaches for his favorite toy or race-crawls to the new one you bought to try to help him feel better.

And you feel the triumph of knowing you nursed your baby back to health and life. You knew what to do all after all.

Now if only you can do it the next time, too.

The politics of mother's milk

July 24, 1989

There's nothing like breast feeding a baby to put you in touch with how underdeveloped our highly developed society is when it comes to human instinct.

In many countries around the world, mothers instinctively bind babies to their chests soon after they're born. The closeness provides the baby warmth, security and the opportunity to suckle at will. Mothers nurse their babies for two years and more, like their mothers before them and theirs before them. The rest of the family goes about its business, while mother and child go about theirs.

Here in the United States, it's almost unnatural to breast feed. Forget instinct.

Women today are the daughters and granddaughters of women who were liberated by formula, a revolutionary milk substitute that allowed women to put their breasts back inside their dresses and get back to the kitchen or the factory.

Many of today's women have never seen anyone breast feed. The're faced with the possibility of their own inadequacy and something even more menacing: disapproval. People stare. Husbands are repulsed.

Even medical professionals, despite knowing the benefits of breast feeding, often discourage women from breast feeding when they report routine complications such as slow milk production.

This sometimes is the result of ignorance: a 1993 study by the Sheps Center for Health Services Research in Chapel Hill, N.C., found that among a group of 5,000 resident and practicing physicians, 23 percent of pediatricians, 31 percent of family physicians and 54 percent of OB-GYNs attended no breast feeding lectures during residency. Further, anecdotal research by the Sheps Center suggests that doctors who know the least about breast feeding are doctors who are least comfortable with the act; many are the husbands and sons of women who didn't breast feed.

The irony is that we are sophisticated enough today to appreciate the qualities of breast milk, which haven't been matched despite 60 years of attempts by formula manufacturers. Unlike formula, for example, breast milk passes along the mother's immunities to the baby and contains enzymes to aid in fat digestion. Health organizations such as the American Academy of Pediatrics say the ideal diet for a baby is breast milk only for the first six months of life and breast milk as a supplement for the next six months.

Having read during my pregnancy of these benefits and others, to include low cost and convenience, I decided to try nursing. With the help of a lactation nurse, my baby latched on within a few hours after he was born. But a week later, I began suffering painful breast infections. My obstetrician treated me with antibiotics for the first infection. But when I phoned him to report a second infection at two weeks postpartum, he suggested that I consider weaning.

By that time I was determined. I was spurred on, partly I think by an unnamed urge to rebel, but mostly because I knew breast feeding was best for my baby. What's more, I liked it. It was easy. It was convenient. I'd also offhandedly discovered there's nothing like looking into the face of your child as you give yourself to him.

I told my doctor I'd think about what he said, but I instead picked up the phone and called a breast feeding support organization I'd heard about called La Leche League. Within five minutes I was talking with a mother who'd nursed four babies. During the next several months, she and other women taught me the nuances of breast feeding that nobody else would or could, including how to stave off future infections by massaging clogged milk ducts and taking care of myself.

Today, despite early warnings from a trusted doctor, I continue to supplement Christopher's diet with my milk, even as he approaches his 10-month birthday and disapproving friends and relatives want to know when I'm going to wean.

I continue, only with the guidance of women who have gone before me. I continue because I'm lucky enough to be married to a husband who isn't particularly awestruck, but neither does breast feeding repulse him. I have a boss who lets me take long lunches so I can go home and nurse the baby.

I feel I'm a stronger woman as a result of this experience, which forced me to find my convictions and stay with them.

I'm also angry to the point of being militant. This isn't just about breast feeding. This is about individual choice. This is about doctors who don't listen to women and who don't know how to direct them. This is about people who shame a woman for breast feeding in public and thus shame her very instincts. Our country might lead the world in military might and free enterprise, but it doesn't have a clue about what a woman's body is for.

I'm angry when I hear about how other cultures accept a woman's nature–not just in the Third World, but in England, where at an airport in

London, there is a quiet room with overstuffed chairs. The sign on the out-side reads "Nursing Mothers."

I'm angry at employers who are too embarrassed to discuss breast feed-ing with new mothers who might only need to ask for a room where they can pump milk for their baby.

I'm angry, when, after all these months, one of the nurses at my pediatri-cian's office walked into the examination room where Christopher and I were waiting for his 9-month checkup, and announced, "We like our moth-ers to stop breast feeding by one year."

Funny, I thought it was up to the mother and child to decide when to wean. But maybe that was just my instincts telling me that.

When work and babies collide

Oct. 23, 1989

Seven days after a hurricane struck the coast of South Carolina, my baby turned 1. And while my newspaper colleagues worked their seventh 10- or 12- or 15-hour day without a break, I took the day off to spend his birthday with him.

Two years ago, I would have fully participated in my newspaper's cover-age of the worst natural disaster in South Carolina history.

This was the kind of story I thrived on. If there was a disaster, I wanted to be in the middle of it. If there was human emotion, I wanted to record it. Whatever it took to get the story, long hours, nights away from home, you could count on me.

When I found out I was pregnant, it dawned on me that work couldn't be the end-all anymore. And as the baby growing inside became more real, I began to think it might be time to leave the adrenalin surges to someone else. The absolute way out would have been to quit work, but with a husband in graduate school, that option was never considered.

I decided to switch jobs, to leave the news-writing staff, which is driven by everyday events, and to join the feature/lifestyle staff, which at my news-paper operated at a much slower pace.

Unlike my job as a news reporter when I didn't know when a car accident might have me working until 11 p.m., a feature-writing job would be more predictable. I could leave work at a predetermined hour in the evening and relieve the sitter on time, most of the time. I could take lunch breaks, which would allow me to be with my son at a midway point every day. If I had to leave work in the middle of the day for some reason, I could make up the hours the next day or later that night after Christopher was in bed.

I could be mother first. Working woman second.

I could do things like take the day off on my baby's birthday.

And such a beautiful birthday it was.

I spent the first part of the morning on the phone with my sister, reminiscing about Christopher's birth and his first year.

It is amazing, isn't it, sister, that the bundle I brought home a year ago already has six teeth and seven words?

How he fascinates us, perched as he is somewhere between dependence and independence.

He arches his back to get out of my lap, then whines to get back in.

He races up every set of steps he sees, then waits for me to take him down.

He crawls and stands alone briefly, but needs Mommy to hold his hands when he wants to scout out a room on foot.

On his birthday day, Christopher and I hung balloons for his party. We went to lunch, where we proudly announced to other diners, "Today is our first birthday." We combed a book store, looking for too many books to give him.

At his party that night, most of Christopher's favorite people were there. He got cake all over his face and way too many presents. And when it was over, he rolled around on our bed, wired and happy, until 10:30 p.m., when he fell asleep, cackling with joy.

It was an uncompromisingly beautiful birthday day full of memory-making moments.

And then I went back, to post-Hugo Day 8, to a newsroom full of dedicated reporters pounding keyboards, shouting into phones and looking as if they had never left the office or their commitment to newspapering. They had been there the day before, too, working late into the night on the biggest story of their lives while I was home giving my first baby his first birthday party.

Walking back into that newsroom that day, I encountered feelings I didn't know were there.

I love my son. I knew that already. I knew that he will always come first.

What I didn't know, what I learned that day when I walked back into the hub, is that I won't always feel so unfaltering about my new priority.

People often idolize the image of the dedicated reporter dropping everything to get the story, but not the idea of the dedicated working mother dropping everything to give her baby a birthday party.

Not even me.

Holding on to the afternoon light

Feb. 5, 1990

Unaware of my presence, he stood quiet in the filmy afternoon light, studying a tree where a bird was singing.

His little corduroy pants, too long, were rolled up above his fat shoes. His sweater was too small, his T-shirt too big. His hand was outstretched toward the bird.

Then he saw me. He turned toward me and squinted into the sun, showing me his seven teeth. And he ran away on 16-month-old legs, cackling, daring me to chase him, his fists beating the air in perfect sync with each wobbly step.

"This is my favorite age," I think these days.

But then I said the same thing a month ago and the month before and the month before that.

Each stage of my firstborn's life has brought new joy.

A first crawl, a first step, a lift of the head, a laugh, a new word, something always to keep me amazed, amused, in awe. There's always been something, and I've had to wonder how it is that I will one day fall out of love with him.

How is it that parents of teenagers say, "You'd better enjoy him while he's young"? How is it that the mother of a 6-year-old, even, once looked at me wistfully and said, "That is such a good age. Enjoy it."?

I've not wanted to hear such comments, but have chosen instead to believe that I will be different, that with every stage Christopher enters, I will think, "This has got to be my favorite age."

I've wanted to believe that if I cling tenaciously, I can hang on to the joys of parenting, always be as in love with mothering as I am now.

Right now, there's little room for complication. He is as pure and sweet as honey, a babbling brook of nonsense and animal noises, an acquiescent partner on Saturday mornings when the rest of the neighborhood is sleeping in. He is 16 months new, just waking up to the world. I love being with him, watching him.

What's more, he loves being with me.

I am the first one he looks for in a crowded room, and his primary teacher. Right now, he doesn't question what I say. Right now, he trusts me completely. He doesn't even know to defy me yet.

Soon he'll reach out to other people and things. He will learn to say, "No, Mommy!" One day he might even say, "You're mean, Mommy" or "I don't like you, Mommy."

One day he won't let me chase him in the afternoon light.

I guess this is what those other mothers mean. It's not that they don't love their grown-up children or that they want to quit being parents or even that parenting becomes more of a burden or a disappointment as children grow older.

It's just that they remember the afternoon light, too, when life was pure and their baby was in love.

Want Dad involved, Mom? Stifle yourself.

March 5, 1990

My husband used to appear happiest with fatherhood when he was tossing Christopher in the air.

Tossing was what they had.

With many thanks to me, tossing was about all they had, as I was constantly reminding Steve that because he was the father, he couldn't possibly know how to do anything else.

The irony was that I wanted Steve to take care of the baby.

But Steve couldn't do anything right. Don't hold Christopher that way. Don't put that much food on his spoon. You've put the diaper on too tight again.

To my credit, barking had validity at times, like when Steve put Christopher on the changing table, then left the room to retrieve the wipes as Christopher's whirling legs prepared to propel him to the floor.

Still, I'm sure my female superiority kept Steve from participating more fully.

I tried to control my urges. But I couldn't control them any more than my husband can control his urge to toss a baby in the air.

Clearly, I'm not alone on this one.

"I give a lot of talks on fatherhood and parenting," James Levine, director of The Fatherhood Project at New York's Families and Work Institute, told me. "This is, without doubt, THE issue."

"Without fail, a woman in the audience will raise her hand and say, 'I want my husband to help, and he won't.' Some man leaps up and gives a rejoinder, 'I want to be involved, but my wife won't let me.'"

Levine blames the conflict on the times. Mothers today know they can and should ask fathers for help. But they continue to harbor haunting memories of their own mothers doing it all.

"It's a real setup," says Levine, whose fatherhood project is dedicated to getting fathers more involved in child rearing. "He (the father) gets involved, whether it's changing, feeding, giving the bath. He gets criticized for doing it his way. He backs off. He hides behind the newspaper. She (the mother) says 'See! You don't want to share. You're not involved.' "

Alas and alack, Levine says many moons will pass before men are automatically given equal time in the nursery.

"Worlds don't change that easily," Levine concluded.

And yet there are steps, Levine says, that my husband and I can take to change things in our own home.

First: We should be aware we're not alone. This is a universal parent trap. Check.

Second: I should acknowledge to Steve how hard this is for me. Double check.

Third: I should bite my tongue. Ouch.

"If you (the mother) really want him (the father) to be involved, then you can't keep giving him negative feedback or criticism," Levine says.

In all fairness to mother instinct, Levine concedes fathers do have a tendency to be rough or overly adventurous with children. And mothers have every right to step in when they do.

But in the everyday give-and-take, Mommy needs to let go if she ever wants Daddy to play a part.

I'm trying to take Levine's advice. This doesn't always work. I still step in where I'm not really needed. Steve still backs off when I do.

And yet, it's true, the more I let go, the more he gets involved. And the more he gets involved, the more automatic involvement is. The more automatic involvement is, the more responsibility is shared.

Everybody wins.

Daddy finds fatherhood can be more than roughhousing and discipline. Mommy gets time to do other things.

And our son learns that sharing domestic responsibilities is what he's going to be expected to do, too.

The serious business of having babies

March 19, 1990

My husband and I are negotiating a second child.

We finally decided we want one. Now we have to decide when. It's a delicate debate about a delicate subject, with solid arguments on both sides.

My arguments:

1) I turn 35 in a few months. Despite continuing encouragement from the medical profession—that women over 30 can deliver as healthy a baby as their younger counterparts—the "over 35" label still wears like a scarlet letter. Doctors still advise the over-35 pregnant woman to have an amniocentesis and to beware of a much greater chance of infertility and miscarriage.

2) Christopher turns 3 in September. Family analysts say the first baby should be at least 3 before you have the second baby. They used to say 2 was good. But now they say there's too much sibling rivalry if the gap between children isn't at least three years. And a 2-year-old progressing well at potty training will inevitably revert if he sees little brother or sister's bottom getting all that attention.

Steve's argument:

1) Practicality. This irritating catchall includes such matters as whether we can afford a second baby, whether our house can hold a second baby and whether I will gripe twice as much about the division of labor if we have two children.

My bottom line: I want to have a baby sometime next year, before I turn 36 and just before Christopher turns 3.

His bottom line: He wants to have a baby sometime after the Cubs win the World Series.

I argue that my arguments can't be tampered with. And if practicality enters into the decision, we might never have a second baby.

He argues that all this hype about maternal aging and optimum gaps between children is likely to mean nothing. Practicality is the only tangible argument, he says.

Back and forth across the negotiating table we go, which leads me to daydream about just getting pregnant. Simply having a baby.

What ever happened, anyway, to couples having wild, rampant romps that occasionally sent the wife, unbeknownst to the husband, floating off to the doctor in a summery dress? It happens on all the sitcoms.

"Honey?" the wife says upon her return home, a shy look on her face.

"Yes, dear?" her husband replies as he takes both her hands in his, and sits, in perfect sync with his wife, on their love seat.

"I went to the doctor today," she says, batting her lashes and averting her eyes.

"You did, dear?" he says, sitting closer on the love seat.

"You're going to be a daddy again, dear," she says, as she lifts her eyes to meet his.

He showers her with kisses, just as the child(ren)/cat/dog come running. They all fall together, laughing and kissing and patting Mommy's tummy.

Maybe scenes like these occurred in simpler times. Maybe they occur somewhere in real life now. My hunch is TV made them up.

My hunch, 2 1/2 years into marriage, 17 months into shared parenting and as many months into offspring negotiations, is that for most people, having babies in real life is romantic during select few moments.

Having babies more often is serious business between two participating adults who are aware, at all points, of the implications of their actions.

As well it should be, I suppose. After all, the sitcoms don't show us the next scene, when the father goes on a two-week drinking binge trying to figure out how he's going to feed that darling new mouth.

Still, all this talk of combined household earnings, career status, optimum gaps and equality, not to mention amniocenteses, miscarriages and infertility, makes me awfully tired.

I think I need to go to bed. Dear?

Grandmother

April 16, 1990

My mother, who lives 700 miles from me and my family, flew in last week for an eight-day visit and immediately started telling me what I should do differently. Nicely. I must admit she did it nicely. She talked to me through Christopher.

"Don't you think you need a sweater on your arms, Christopher?"

"Are you sure you want all that milk before you eat your other food, Christopher?"

"Where's your bib, CHRISTOPHER?"

Of course 18-month-old Christopher had no control over any of these things. It is only I who did, at least that week, since my husband conveniently had business out of town during my mother's visit. It is only I who could choose to ignore my mother's first pieces of advice, and then, hours into her visit, decide to comply. She was right. She's always right.

My mother was 9 when she started taking care of babies. That was the way it was in her day. Children took care of children. Extended families took care of extended families. Aunts and uncles, cousins, grandmothers—everybody lived together in the same town, sometimes in the same house, generation after generation.

My mother raised a brother and two sisters, then four of her own girls. There came the only other grandchild, a boy now 12, who used to live around the corner from her but recently moved 850 miles away. All that experience, and she's a nurse, too.

She knew I was putting Christopher's nose drops in wrong.

"Don't you think you should hold his nostrils after you put those in?"

I did it the way she said. And his nose cleared up for the first time in days.

She knew when it was and when it wasn't time for him to go to bed.

"Don't you think he's a little too wired to go to bed just now?" she said to me at 9:40 one night as I plopped on the couch.

From his bedroom came the first strains of crying. At 11, he was still up.

Details. She noticed all the details and nuances I don't have time, or take time, to see.

My mother noticed me, too. She noticed that she's never seen me look so tired. She watched me one morning, throwing clothes around and running in and out of the dining room trying to feed Christopher in between doing my hair before work. She shook her head.

"I don't know how you girls do it these days. I wish I was here to help you," she said, tears forming.

My mother fantasizes a lot about living in the same town with us. She'd work on the weekends and take care of Christopher during the week.

Never mind that she's got her own life there and we've got ours here or that we'd all drive each other crazy after a while.

None of that matters. What matters to her is that families are supposed to be together. Grandmothers and grandchildren weren't meant to be separated any more than mothers and children were meant to be.

She was talking through Christopher again.

"I bet you know I love you about as much as your mama does," she said, laughing and shaking her head back and forth like mothers do to their children. He laughed, too.

Today my mother flew back home, where she lives alone, having divorced several years ago, and where she goes to school to further the nurse's education she couldn't focus on when she was raising her own four children. Her meager student's income won't allow her to fly back here for a long time.

We might see her again in six months. So far, that's been our average. She's seen Christopher three times since he was born, an average of seven days each visit.

I took a lot of pictures while Mama was here. I'll send them to her when they're developed, even though I know what she'll do with them when she gets them.

Just as she does all the pictures I send her, she'll put them in the bottom of a drawer so she won't have to look at them.

A bonfire of parenting books

June 28, 1990

One day soon I'm going to quit reading.

I'm going to give up Rosemond, Spock, Brazelton and all the rest. I'm going to stop weighing what I think might be right against what the "experts" say. I'm going to make decisions on my own.

I tell myself this, but in my quest for the perfect formula to raise the perfect child, I continue to devour all manner of parenting advice.

I have no choice, you see: My name is Mommy.

I'm not the only one. I can hear the rumblings of insecurity when I talk to other mothers about almost any issue in child rearing. We're all worrying about what one expert vs. the other is saying.

And why not? In laboratories across the nation, psychologists are determining the impact of everything on a child's life. If they're not studying serial killers and whether their mothers worked or didn't, they're studying the effects of peanut butter on playground aggression.

Well-meaning mothers, who are still the ones spreading most of the peanut butter, suck up the results of these tests, which jump out at us from the front page of the newspaper, from women's magazines, from placards in the doctor's office.

The irony is, not only do these soundbites of wisdom often not affirm us, they very often shake our instincts to the bone.

When Christopher was 6 months old and the daytime sitter was suggesting that he should be putting himself to sleep without my happily rocking/nursing/singing to him, I went to Dr. William A.H. Sammons for help.

I'd been comfortable with my methods. By helping my baby to sleep, I thought I was helping him feel loved and secure during those first frightening months out of the womb. Mothers in purer, more primitive, cultures keep their babies strapped to their bodies for years. Rocking and singing was the least I could do for mine.

Sammons' book, *The Self-Calmed Baby*, which was passed along to me just as I was beginning to question myself, told me there were important benefits, not the least of which was independence, to letting days-old babies put themselves to sleep.

Sammons' second message, whether intentional or not—read between the lines—was: Mothers who don't let their babies put themselves to sleep will create whiny, dependent adults who never stand on their own feet.

Even articles that don't seek to gang up on us do so unintentionally.

"Mothers: Taking the Rap," an article in *The Sunday New York Times* magazine, looked innocent enough. I applauded the article for its premise, that society unfairly blames mothers for the psychological disorders of their children.

"I say the psychiatric world could still afford to focus less on dissecting and perfecting mothers and more on removing some of the real obstacles (like bad child care) that remain in their paths," wrote clinical social worker Janna Malamud Smith.

But, of course, the phrase in the article that stuck with me was this one: "Schizophrenia is no longer understood only as the product of a mother's intrusive and smothering behavior. (SHE MAY BE A PLAYER but hardly alone on the stage.)"

Forget the fact that the writer appropriately discounted the notion that I will be totally responsible for Christopher seeing a therapist at age 6.

The idea that I could play even a small role was enough. After all, I'd already been branded intrusive and smothering by the author of *The Self-Calmed Baby*.

I've read a lot of other articles that further my fears about the way I mother. I try to stick to my guns. But reading always makes me feel queasy.

So silly. So ironic, that even as I am desperately seeking ways to keep my child sane, I am driving myself crazy.

The truth is that nobody can tell any one mother how to raise any one child. Each special set of circumstances cannot be weighed in one four-page spread in *Parents* magazine or even in a book. I need to recognize the limitations of advice given by "experts," albeit usually well-being, who don't know me.

I know that. I need to pound that into my head. But I won't. I can't. I must keep on cruising the experts, every one I come across.

I have no choice, remember: My name is Mommy.

Toddlerhood: boot camp for lords of discipline

July 26, 1990

Until you have one of your own, it's hard to appreciate that a "toddler" is more than just a child who toddles.

A toddler also is a child who teeters—between good behavior, which will showcase solid parenting skills for the rest of your life, and bad behavior, with which he will stress and shame you during the same time period.

Take sleeping. The infant who used to look so sweet, curled on his tummy in a tiny ball, now looks like something out of *Where the Wild Ones Are* when it's time for bed.

It's not like sleeping is an occasional thing, either. Sleep must be dealt with at least once a day, usually at the end of the day, when you'd rather deal in peaceable interchange than World War III.

Eating is another meeting of the minds. Our 22-month-old, who used to sit so happily in the high chair lapping up whatever we put in front of him, will now sit in the high chair only after attempting to eat from the card table, from the coffee table and from the top of the decorative picnic basket in the kitchen.

While eating dinner at a friend's house, he tossed a fork across the floor, whined because he wanted a tablespoon of salad dressing on each piece of lettuce and squirmed out of his chair three times.

One does not fine-dinner-dine with a toddler, nor even eat lunch downtown.

Real discipline begins during the toddler years. The same child who used to shrink the second you said "No!" now shakes his head back at you, grins that toddler grin and goes right on marching atop the stereo turntable while Daddy's special old records are playing.

Riding in the car becomes a different matter during this special stage of development. The infant who couldn't put his little hands together has grown into a child who can decode the most complicated of car seats. Driving home from work one afternoon this week, I looked into my rearview mirror to see my child standing inches from my ear.

"Hi!" he said, toddler grin in place.

And lest we forget, the need for potty training rears itself during toddlerhood. The implications here are almost too much to bear.

"Parents who neglect toilet training may well be fostering a child who will later exhibit slovenliness, indifference and other undesirable traits," say Donald Helms and Jeffrey Turner in *Exploring Child Behavior.*

The best thing that can be said about toddlers is that they can entertain themselves. Even then, they can't be trusted—particularly if they're being quiet.

Quiet. Perhaps the essence of parenting a toddler can be captured in quiet.

Quiet in a toddler house almost always means something naughty is going on: Toilet paper is being stuffed inside the big people potty. Little hands are eating from the kitty bowl. A body has escaped to the front porch and is preparing to jump.

Quiet in a toddler house almost always means you're going to have to do something parental when you'd much rather take the opportunity to sit there and be quiet for a minute, too.

Baby's first home

Aug. 23, 1990

There is something special about bringing home a baby for the first time.

Standing in the doorway of the baby's room, I can readily recall the mix of feelings.

How safe I felt putting the little bundle in the crib for the first time. How nervous. How proud to lead visitors to his crib to witness the movement of his chest as he breathed. How afraid he would wake up. How peaceful I felt in the excited quiet of the house. How other-worldly.

Walking through other rooms of our first baby's first house, I can easily conjure other first moments as a parent.

There's the corner of the dining room floor where we put his highchair. Seeing that corner, now weathered from scrubbing, I can remember how thrilled I was simply seeing him eat for the first time.

There's the spot in a doorway where he took his first steps, and the one in the living room where he took his first bad fall. I can recall how excited I felt about the one, how fearful about the other.

There's the window in the living room where he liked to be held so he could wave good-bye when we left him with someone else. I can walk over to the window and touch the kiss prints that are still there. I can touch how important I was to him.

I can sit in the house and feel that first winter with him. I remember packing away the tiny summer shirts and bringing out the bulky sweaters that never fit right. How I worried that his little body would be cold in his big, drafty room.

A baby's first house is a special house, a house that holds memories of first struggles that won't ever come again, certainly not with the next child, or the next, when so many things aren't so new anymore.

Last week we left our tiny first house, with its heat grate in the hallway and its portable air conditioners that never got cold enough. We moved into a bigger, more modern place with central air and heat and lots of room for Christopher to run around in.

The new place is full of hope and promise. There will be more special moments with our child. Maybe, one day, a new baby. We are excited about the prospects for our family there.

The old place was just a house.

But it's still empty as it waits for new tenants. I still have the key.

And after work, before I pick up Christopher, I think I'll walk through one more time.

Two fewer enlistees for the mommy wars

Oct. 18, 1990

When I was 19, I met a woman who was as confused about life as I. Our sameness apparent, we attached ourselves to each other during the next few years, ultimately rooming together, working together and enrolling in college together.

We shared the agonies of our early 20s together, and when college was over, we went our separate ways, as college roommates often do.

She moved north. She became a successful real estate agent and married a wealthy entrepreneur. She bought a sports car and a two-story house, which she decorated in the fashionable country style of the New England state where she lives. Her financial status eventually allowed her to quit her job so she could focus on her two children. She got involved with the Junior League.

I stayed in the South. I became a newspaper reporter and married a graduate student. I bought a used car and rented an apartment. I still have some of the furniture I used when Susan and I lived together. I had to go back to work when my baby was 4 months old. I got involved with child care.

Susan and I know these things about each other because we've kept in touch during the eight years we've been apart. Despite the miles between us in geography and lifestyle, the foundation we established in the early days keeps us in frequent contact, by phone and mail.

We share laughter about the past, anxiety about the future and awe over how much we love our children. She has listened to me agonize about my dueling role as mother and professional. I have listened to her talk with certainty about her decision to stay home.

We have our differences, and yet I can't imagine anything coming between us, not even the Mommy Wars, which trend-watchers say Susan and I should be fighting these days: She can choose to stay home. I can't. She's supposed to think I'm a bad mother because I work. I'm supposed to be angry at her for that.

I'm supposed to snipe at her when I phone her in the middle of the day and she's at home, like one stay-home mother reported to *Newsweek* for an article about the politics of motherhood. The phone had rung four times one afternoon before the stay-home mother could get to it. When she finally answered the phone, her working mother friend on the other end of the line, drawled, "Oh, sorry, did I interrupt a crucial moment in your soap opera?"

One stay-home mother did worse than snipe, according to "The Mommy War," an article in *Texas Monthly*. When a working mother she met in a grocery store asked the question, "What do you do?" the stay-home mother hurled a head of lettuce at the enemy and hissed, "I stay home with my children, which is what you should do."

I am not totally inactive in this war. I count among my friends many women who stay home with their children. And while my friends and I do not engage in open warfare with each other, I sometimes find myself battling my own insecurities because of my relationships with them.

I overcompare my child's ability to socialize/count to 10/be polite with their child's ability to do the same. I feel uncomfortable when my friends bring out homemade cakes and chicken pot pies made from scratch.

I participate in the Mommy Wars when I disassociate myself from them from time to time because I can't stand the pain of knowing they can be with their children when I can't be with mine. Sometimes I can feel their pain, too, like when I talk about work with their husbands, and they get quiet or leave the room.

Participation in this war can be as passive as this avoidance, brought on by our own uncertainty and pain.

Susan lately has become uncertain. During a conversation a few days ago, my friend who has for four years spoken so happily of life at home, suddenly announced she was thinking about working a couple of days a week. She has found herself overwhelmed with being a full-time mother to two children, 5 months and 3 years.

"I just feel I'll be a better mother if I can get out of here a little," she said. "It's better for me to be here five days a week, happy, than seven days a week miserable."

Susan is certain that she wants to work only part time, maybe 15 or 20 hours a week.

She's uncertain about leaving her children with someone else.

"They're going to learn someone else's values," she said, her voice dropping off.

Susan shares the pain of choice, just as I share with her the pain of no choice.

We hold each other up. And as time passes, we continue to find we have more in common than we have differences: We share an intense love for our children and a tremendous pressure to do the right thing.

We also know we need each other.

We need each other way too much to do battle.

Mothers know

Nov. 1, 1990

Waiting in line at a restaurant with my 2-year-old and a friend the other day, I was disappointed to discover the presence of a dirty diaper and the absence of a clean replacement.

I told my friend we'd have to cancel our long-awaited lunch date as the nearest diaper store was several minutes away.

Then I saw her: Another mother with her baby.

I marched right over to her table and reported our predicament. She didn't hesitate either but went straight to her car and got a diaper for me. She waved away my offer to pay.

"I know how it is," she said.

Single women, especially those who find peace without a man, are special creatures. Fathers, most notably the ones who pour apple juice on demand, are marvelous people. Married women without children are great, as are bachelors and little girls and boys.

But mothers are solidarity.

Only we know that we can tell much longer stories about giving birth than having sex and that underneath our clothes are bodies that will never be the same again no matter what we tell our husbands.

Only we know what we will do for our children.

A mother will do whatever it takes.

A mother will allow a baby to throw half his food on the floor if that's what it takes to get the other half in his mouth. A mother will share her Popsicle with a slobbery toddler, use the bottom of her shirt to wipe a chocolate face as it heads off to an important occasion, and set the alarm for 5:30 a.m. because she forgot she promised homemade cupcakes for her kindergartner's class tomorrow. A mother whose child is sick will hold out her hands if she can't find a towel and stand like a statue in the middle of the night making sure a wheezing chest continues to move up and down.

In the area of pediatric nursing, in fact, there is no rival. I know of one mother whose son had terrible asthma, who slept in her son's room every night for six years because she was afraid she wouldn't hear him begin an attack. When she finally decided he needed to sleep alone for his own emotional well-being, she moved to the floor outside his room.

I do not mean to discredit fathers. They are critical legs on the family tripod. But despite their increased contributions in the domestic arena, mothers still have the market on primary caretaking, marked by strong responses.

Some sociologists say these responses are biological. Others suggest our urges come from centuries of socialization, beginning with an earlier way of life; hunters/men couldn't slay bison with babies strapped on their backs, but gatherers/women could sow seed and pick maize with a baby.

Whatever the reason—and however much it needs to change—the urge to respond like lightning to the cry in the night and to take early note of the dirty diaper during the day—or at least be the first to take the baby to the changing table—continues to be stronger among the general mother population. So is the urge among mothers to help each other.

I still remember with great comfort the family gatherings at my grandmother's house when women in big dresses and red lipstick stood in circles, talking secretly among themselves. Over the years, I'd watch as newly married aunts and cousins shyly joined the circle.

I never knew what they were whispering about in there. Now I know that they were talking about the cycles of life. They were teaching and learning, pulling each other along in there.

Standing just outside the circle and looking in, I felt a sense of security, but also a longing to belong.

Now I do. Now I find that the circle reaches beyond the walls of my grandmother's house to include best friends who live in other states, strangers with diapers and a mother who saw my 2-year-old bring down a rack of gum as we were preparing to leave the store the other night.

"We've all been there," she said, as she bent to help.

Jogging baby buggy—a Rockwell for the '90s?

Nov. 15, 1990

Driving through a tree-lined neighborhood on my way home from work recently, I saw a jogger rushing down the street with one of those baby buggies for runners.

I scowled, like I always do at such blatant displays of my generation's style of parenting.

But the jogger's face looked grim as he struggled to exercise and spend quiet time with his blonde toddler, equally poker-faced in her bouncing buggy seat high above bicycle-sized tires. He didn't look happy with any of what he was doing.

I felt sorry then, not just for him; this scene might be the personification of so many families today, driven as we are by a lack of time and child care. There's never enough of either.

I'm sure there's never been enough and that parents have always been afraid as they make decisions about raising children. But yesterday's parenting fears have been compounded today by an overwhelming lack of support and a fear that the way we're doing things is horribly wrong.

You hear it all the time. The once supportive extended family, which might have been available during another generation to baby-sit that baby girl while her father jogged, has just about disintegrated. Community networking has been eroded by crime. Today's parents get advice out of books, support from psychologists and contraptions out of catalogs.

Parents today are haunted, by the homey—and unreachable—image of childhood they grew up knowing in the aberrant 1950s, and by modern-day studies reporting everything bad that could possibly happen to children because of the way we're raising them. (How many times can we hear that children watch an average 25 hours of TV every week and that they will see 52,000 attempted murders by the time they're 18?)

People wonder why parents in the 1990s whine so much. This is why.

"Parents are not raising their children the way they themselves were raised," Philip Elmer-DeWitt wrote for *Time* magazine's "The Great Experiment." "None have any idea how it will turn out. And all live in perpetual fear that some piece of their carefully crafted child-care structure will fall out of place and bring the fragile edifice of their lives tumbling down like a toddler's tower of blocks."

There does exist the antithesis of the jogger's way of life, in Norman Rockwell paintings and sometimes in reality. I saw it once, when I interviewed a South Carolina farm family for a story I was doing on farm life.

The father didn't have to jog to stay lean and healthy. He worked from sunup to sundown. So did the mother and the two boys, 14 and 17, when they weren't in school.

Nobody in that family had to be taught that hard work pays off. The boys had played a deciding role in the family's economic status for years. Nobody had to be taught values. Values were lived.

Society's ills have to be fought off there like they do everywhere, but community and family are strong.

I could spend my days pining away for that way of life, so different from the lives of men and women in tortoise-shell glasses hurrying home from work so they can hurry down the street, bewildered children in tow.

The problem is, neither the farm culture, nor the 1950s culture, is available to most of us.

That doesn't mean we should quit whining. Some things need to be changed in this country, inadequate child care for one.

But, as a friend suggested one day when I was worrying whether my children could thrive without a stay-home mother and a grandmother down the street, we can't keep pining away for what we can't have anymore.

Some of today's societal makeup, like the mobile, two-income family, is probably here to stay. We need to take what we can from those simpler times and let go of the rest. We need to move on.

We also need to quit judging each other. Life is alienating and complicated enough.

If a man finds he can make his way by jogging with his child, bravo.

During those 1950s about which we are so nostalgic, he probably wouldn't have been caught dead with his hand on a baby buggy.

Take good care of my baby

Feb. 27, 1991

I used to only read about people like the New Jersey mother who told *Newsweek* for a story on child care that she went through nine child-care situations before her baby was 2.

I never imagined I'd be like her.

Then my son's first caregiver moved, and his second quit when she got pregnant. A third caregiver didn't want to keep children past a certain age. And we left a fourth caregiver when we realized that her philosophies were decidedly different from our own.

We liked the fifth arrangement, in a small church center that had just opened. But last month, a sixth arrangement, one of those established child-care centers with a waiting list, called with a vacant slot. Christopher's name had been on the list for 25 months. And when his name came up, we felt we had no choice but to leave No. 5, which had become grossly overcrowded, and take on respected, established No. 6.

Certainly not all parents are like us.

I know one couple who managed right away to get their firstborn in one of the best child care-centers, which in our town is defined by a waiting list of 200 or more. The couple got their child moved to the top of the waiting list by changing not only churches, but denominations; the church-run center gives priority to children of church members.

I know another couple who were lucky enough to place their second infant in a similar child-care program as soon as they needed child care. They accomplished this by delaying the second pregnancy until they knew their first child was firmly established in the program; like church members, siblings also are given priority status on waiting lists.

I also am acquainted with parents who avoid waiting lists and child-care hopping by leaving their children in places that are adequate enough.

Between arrangement Nos. 2 and 3, I toured one child-care center that looked nice enough on the outside. Inside, it was dark and dank, and in the middle of a group of children sat a big square box with a gate and wooden bars for walls. The gate was locked, and a boy of about 6 was sitting in there with his head in his hands. The director called this vault "time-out."

In another room, I saw what looked tiny cages with latched gates built into the wall. I later learned that cribs like these are manufactured for infant use only; they're too small for older children. Also, an older child might feel caged while an infant wouldn't know the difference.

These particular "cribs" were filled with 2- and 3-year-old children. The gates were locked shut with lengths of rags. I was told the children had been put there because they wouldn't stay in their playpens during naptime. The cribs were so small the children had to keep their legs bent to fit. The children, even then awake despite their caregivers' intent, stared out at me as I walked past.

There was another center that my husband and I thought about touring between child-care arrangement No. 1 and No. 2 and again between 2 and 3. This little house had playground equipment in the front yard, children in and out all day long and a marquee advertising child care for $25 a week. We figured something was wrong with child care that cost a third of the going rate. And so we never checked it out. And then one day driving by, we noticed the children were gone.

I found out later that the center was shut down because of continuous regulatory violations, including grossly inadequate space and staffing.

Yet during the trial, parent after parent testified on behalf of the child-care center. They couldn't be concerned that their children weren't getting the care they deserved.

"We don't want our affordable child care taken away. Where are we going to go?" the parents beseeched.

This is not to suggest that all child-care facilities are bad, that all child-care workers have evil intent or that all parents have bad experiences with child care. This is to suggest that we are living in a country with a scarcity of child care that is dependable, affordable and good. This is to suggest an irony: The economic atmosphere is such in this country that both parents must work to make ends meet. Yet, according to the Child Care Action Campaign, we live in the only industrialized nation besides South Africa whose government doesn't guarantee free or subsidized, standardized child care to its citizens.

This is to suggest that being the working parent of young children is living on the edge of a pendulum that won't quit moving.

Today, I am not as worried about my child. I am not afraid that my boss is going to start wondering who I'm whispering to on the phone as I go in search of yet another child-care center.

Today, I have good child care.
But what about tomorrow?

The truth about children

March 14, 1991

Children teach their parents many truths without even knowing they're doing it.

There's the truth about sleep. By the time a child quits waking you with nightmares and ear infections, he's a teen-ager out with the car, and you're waking with your own bad dreams. Truth is: Once you become a parent, you wonder if you'll ever catch up on your sleep again.

There's the truth about promises. All those vows you make during the headiness of pregnancy—"I will never give my child cookies to keep him quiet, use the TV as a baby sitter or let him wear a Ninja Turtle T-shirt"—mean nothing as soon as your child learns to scream for any of the above.

There's the truth about important people. Bert is the tall one, and Ernie is the orange one. And the truth about crayons: They were made to be broken and replaced.

There's one very startling truth: The same people who swore to be one way have become another.

The same people who used to be radical non-materialists become parents obsessed with making more than enough money so they can buy their children tennis shoes that light up. The same people who used to make fun of their parents for over-cautious driving become moms and dads who drive just like theirs did. Avowed agnostics 15 years ago teach Sunday school today.

Truth is: You become one of "them."

Some of us were ready. Some were always ready for the increased structure, stability and conservatism that being a parent encourages. For others, the truth comes fast and scary, signifying the loss of youth, which is clung to and mourned over for years.

All of us, if we're lucky, gain understanding.

Finally, we get to know what our own parents meant when they clucked their tongues at some disappointing behavior or other, heaved that great martyr sigh and said, "Just wait until you have children."

My mother used to say this after I moved away from home, every time I let too many days lapse between phone calls to her. Used to be, I'd roll my eyes.

Used to be when I looked at pictures of me and my three sisters, particularly one memorable collection taken after our every-Sunday drive to the mountains, I'd look only to see how cute we were. I didn't think what my parents went through to get four children, ages 1 to 6, dressed, in the station wagon and up the mountain without throwing up.

Now, as I fight to get one 2-year-old to wear something other than his Ninja Turtle T-shirt, I think not only about those weekend outings, but my parents' commitment to get us to church every Sunday, satisfied at Christmas, fed every night, raised.

I also know now the range of their emotions. How helpless you feel to watch a sick offspring in pain. How disappointed, when your pride and joy throws a tantrum in an important person's living room. How you hurt when your child's bare knees land on concrete.

I know, too, that there's no greater joy than getting a sloppy kiss in the morning, a hug after discipline, a story told by your very own, pie-eyed child.

One day a long time ago, I must have been the center of my parents' universe. They must have fidgeted over me and tried to be perfect.

I still catch them trying, like when they try to teach me how to teach my child all the things they realized they should have taught me. They still worry about what they did right and what they did wrong and whether I'm reaping the benefits or suffering the consequences.

Once a parent, always a parent.

Now that I am one, I appreciate that. They always told me I would.

It took a child of my own to make the truth stick.

How many toys can one kid have?

March 28, 1991

I'd been anxious for some time about the number of toys in our house. Unlike most of Christopher's little friends, we don't have the plastic slide, the plastic kitchen or the plastic car.

I thought surely we were depriving him until I mentioned this concern to my mother who, upon visiting his room, promptly pronounced, "YOU DON'T THINK THIS IS ENOUGH TOYS?"

So his room is home to 36 stuffed animals, 68 books, two tricycles and two rocking horses. So he has five shovels, five jigsaw puzzles, 10 cars, five trains, three planes and hundreds of crayons and blocks.

To someone like my mother, a product of the Great Depression who sent her children to the backyard with only a bucket for picking blackberries, this is a lot of toys.

To many of the parents I know, we might be guilty of child neglect.

I have a friend who is a Discovery toy saleswoman. Her formal dining room isn't really a dining room. It is a toyarama. Every possible size, shape and color of toy is stacked on three-tiered shelves lining the walls. Baskets of teeny, tiny plastic things that fit in a farm or a zoo or on some pegboard or another, stacks and stacks of puzzles and stack cups, piles of plastic people and animals all are open to the wandering, wondering eyes and fingers of her children. This is not to mention a full-sized teepee, an aquarium, the plastic kitchen, the plastic slide AND the car in the kids' bedroom.

In my mother's eyes and in the eyes of many people of her generation, my friend's home is overstimulating, overindulging and guilty of discouraging the use of imagination.

In the eyes of many parents today, such homes are stimulating, loving and keeping up with the little Joneses. And I'm just barely keeping up.

How did this generational difference evolve?

Sociologists and psychologists have many theories, some of them defined by words with which we're all too familiar: guilt and commercialization.

Parents today feel bad because they don't spend as much time with their children as their own parents did, etc., etc., and so they pile on the presents, etc., etc. Parents today are lured by advertisements that encourage them to buy.

This phenomenon is well known in toy circles. A marketing business once held a seminar for toy companies. Its honest-to-goodness premise: "How to play off parental guilt to promote the sale of toys to parents."

As if this weren't enough, well-meaning articles about child development in parents' magazines further coerce us:

"Climbing helps the child becoming attuned to and secure with her body," translates to "Please go buy a big plastic slide."

"The child needs to maneuver and manipulate" means "please purchase a motorized car."

"Motor coordination is important" becomes "Pile the toy box with teeny, tiny things."

That Americans buy A LOT of toys for the collective population is a given. The Toy Manufacturers Association said $13.4 billion worth of toys were sold in one year in the United States at the beginning of this decade, more than triple the amount of sales 15 years before.

Determining what is "a lot" for one individual child is not so easy to determine.

Some toys are educational, important for the development of the child, even necessary. But choices have to be made, and because every child is different, these choices can only be made from an individual frame of reference.

My frame of reference tells me I'll keep buying him books and puzzles just because I like going to bookstores with him and buying him books and puzzles. But after what I saw him doing the other day, I don't think I need to buy him the slide.

He pulled a chair up to his old crib and climbed over. He bounced up and down a couple of times. Then he climbed onto the old changing table next to the crib and lowered himself to the ground.

Voilà. It was the best kind of discovery toy.

The rosebush

May 9, 1991

My dad gave me a yellow rosebush after Christopher was born.

I'd never planted anything outside, especially something as delicate as a rose, especially something my green-thumbed father gave me. I was afraid I wouldn't be able to keep it alive.

But with guidance from my father, a farmer's son who thrived among his flowers and vegetables, I got it into the ground.

And with Daddy's patient guidance, grown more patient over the years, the bush flourished.

It was a little thing, but I was proud.

The rosebush was the only thing of beauty growing in our backyard, wild and tangled as it was with weeds and vines.

It was the first thing Christopher watched grow out of the dirt, and I liked putting his baby's nose in the petals so he could smell their fragrance and feel their tenderness.

My father was proud, too. I'd always admired his ability to grow things, and he knew it. Now he was passing along his art to his grown daughter, much like he passed along wide hands, curly hair and blue eyes through me to his grandson.

There were mistakes. Failing to ask Daddy's guidance, I almost suffocated the rosebush one frosty night when I covered the whole thing in a plastic bag to protect it from the cold, instead of pruning the bush and piling dirt on its base like I later learned I should.

Somehow the bush came back. And for two seasons, the bush grew big yellow roses. I was pleased during occasional long-distance conversations to talk with Daddy about the bush and how it grew. I could tell he was pleased, too.

One day last summer, my husband and I moved. We were glad to get out of our first little house and into a big apartment and didn't think much about leaving the rosebush behind. The new tenants loved yellow roses and thought the bush an omen that they should buy the house.

They loved yellow roses so much that I thought I would love to leave the bush with them. Until a few weeks ago when I knew I had to have it.

At first the tenants didn't want to give up the rosebush. It was theirs now, and if I wanted it, I should have come for it a long time ago.

When I told them my reason for wanting it, they softened. And just as one day I dug a hole and planted the hard ball of roots into the earth, they let me dig again.

Only this time I didn't have Daddy's advice to go on.

This time, the robust nature lover, the man my 2½-year-old calls "Poppy," was dying of cancer. He didn't have the strength to talk about anything, much less Sevin dust and peat moss and how you have to cut blooming rose-bushes to nothing when you transplant.

Despite the absence of my father's guiding hand and knowing full well that rosebushes don't do well when they're moved, I dug up the bush in its full spring bloom, chopped its blossoms off and took the bare sticks to a friend's house with a nice big yard.

Christopher watched while I dug a hole, and then he helped pat dirt around the bush with the wide hands my father passed on to him.

"Poppy's plant?" he asked.

"Poppy's plant," I said.

They say rosebushes are delicate, and for a long time I wouldn't go back for fear that I had killed it.

Then a few days ago, a week after my father died of the terminal illness that killed him so quickly, Christopher and I went back to the spot where we planted the yellow rosebush.

From the street, all I could see were bare sticks coming up out of the ground.

Carrying Christopher from the car, I walked closer, and together, we dis-covered tender leaves sprouting out of the sticks. He didn't understand the significance. But I did.

And one day we'll sit by the living rose, and we'll talk.

Cinderella and other lies

May 23, 1991

Children's classics are taking a politically correct beating like everything else these days.

Consider *Dumbo*. There's little to complain about at first glance, only Dumbo's mommy hugging her new baby elephant, a parade of giraffes, seals and tigers preparing for the circus.

Then you get to the part where Dumbo's mommy gets put away for terrorizing the little boy who makes fun of her son's ears.

"Dumbo Mommy cage?" my 2½-year-old asks every time.

"Yes, the animal keeper put Dumbo's Mommy in a cage."

"Why?" he says, his little brow all wrinkled.

Here's where generations of parents explain that Mrs. Jumbo is getting her just punishment for misbehaving. Those of us in the current generation, meanwhile, can't answer the question until we analyze the scene for hidden agendas. Just what does Dumbo say about animal rights?

As a kid, I loved *Hansel and Gretel*.

As a mother, the first time Christopher and I got to the part where Gretel kicks the witch in the oven and shuts the door, I wanted to slam shut the book. I wasn't sure whether I should continue subjecting my child to this kind of behavior or to that of *Sleeping Beauty*'s Prince Charming when he k-i-l-l-s the witch-turned-dragon or how to act when I get to the part where a little red-suited girl's grandmother gets eaten by a wolf.

I have been equally nonplused to see Cinderella finding paradise in the arms of another Prince Charming but delighted to say I've found a way around this tale. I simply forgo the "happily ever after" ending and make up my own.

"He rescues her, but she rescues him, too, because he's very lonely and needs somebody to help him sort out his feelings," I tell Christopher. Or, "They get married, but she probably gets a job, and that makes her happy, too."

Inside children's books are women who are witches, women who let their hair down so some guy can climb up and stepmothers who act like demons possessed. Little pigs put cauldrons of hot water in fireplaces for wolves to fall into. Apples and spindles (whatever those are) drip with poison. And Bambi's mother dies.

These are the books we all grew up reading. Now, according to Dr. Bette Goldstone, many conscientious parents are abandoning the classics because, like me, they don't like Jack breaking his crown or Rock-A-Bye's baby falling to certain death in a windstorm. Goldstone, a professor of education at Beaver College in Glenside, Pa., surveyed the parents of nursery school students to discover that some of them didn't understand words like "tuffet" and "curds and whey."

Goldstone and others say this is a shame.

"They're part of our common culture," says Dr. Jill Locke, outgoing chairwoman of the Caldecott Committee, which is responsible for picking a best-illustrated children's book every year. "These are things people mention all the time in common conversation. I have a friend who married a man with an M.D. He'd never read *Mother Goose*. She made him read *Mother Goose* before they got married. He said 'Oh, geez, this is what people read?' People use children's literature in humor or satire. You have to know it."

Cultural heritage or not, I must admit I have considered ridding Christopher's room of the books that don't balance race, sex, peace, love and color schemes in the bathroom.

But of the dozens upon dozens of books that Christopher owns, the ones he consistently asks Mommy and Daddy to read are the ones that house the difficult issues. They're the ones that he questions, that force us to consider the lessons we want him to learn. Take *Cinderella*.

"Stepmother mean," he says every time he hears the story.

"The stepmother is mean," I say, quickly remembering to add that of course all step people aren't mean.

"Why stepmother mean?"

"Some people are just mean, but people shouldn't be mean, which reminds me if anybody is ever mean to you, you should come tell Mommy and Daddy."

As a child, I read most of the classics: *Dumbo*, *Cinderella*, *Snow White*, all of the Grimm brothers' fairy tales and *Pinocchio* with its very serious message about bad boys, difficult choices and wretched ramifications.

I wasn't brainwashed.

And anyway, if I ever took those books away from Christopher, I'd have to tell him why.

Or I'd have to lie. And then my nose would grow long.

Pinocchio said so.

A *mother's business*

June 6, 1991

My 2½-year-old son has a friend. I know she's his friend because she hugs him when he gets to child care every day and because his eyes light up when her name is mentioned.

I don't know much else about her. I don't know what it is about her that he likes, or, come to think of it, why he seems to favor little girls in general.

I wouldn't mind knowing.

But my business these days is to stay out of his.

Time was, my business was to feed him every spoonful he ate and not let him out of my sight. I was to rock him to sleep as I sang "Hush, Little Baby" and to close the door quietly behind me after I'd carefully laid him in his crib.

Now my business is letting him get the milk jug out of the refrigerator even though he almost topples over trying to get it to the kitchen counter. It's listening to him shout "Go 'way!" when he wants to have a private conversation and "No close door!" at my back as I leave him in his big-boy bed.

Just weeks ago I was picking him up from child care every afternoon and delighting in his stories of the day.

With all the ums, false starts and jibber jabber of someone just learning language, he'd tell me what he ate for lunch and whether he played outside.

He'd talk to me about his little playmates, especially the little girl, and whether they sang "I'm a Little Teapot" and "Itsy-Bitsy Spider."

Sometimes, he'd even perform for me as we drove home, putting his thumb and forefinger together to make the spider climb up the water spout.

Now when I ask him what he did on any given day he says, "No! No talk!"

My business now is knowing he has secrets and letting him have them.

His business is dragging the white foot stool from the sink in the kitchen to the sink in the bathroom, even though there's already a blue one in there.

No reason. Or maybe there is, I just don't know it. Heaven forbid I should ask.

His business is getting mad when he can't make something move, gloating when he gets undressed for his bath all by himself and giggling hysterically when I stub my toe.

My business is labeling his emotions and then stepping aside.

His business is turning the TV on when it's time and off when it's time and trying to turn it on and off many times in between. His business is brushing the air inside his mouth instead of his teeth and bouncing on his bed but only in the middle because I make it my business to keep him from falling off.

His business is secrets, mysteries and a burning desire to become independent—in short, childhood.

My business, now and forevermore, is picking my arguments.

Sociologists say a child's relationship with his parents is primary. The relationship remains primary as children sniff out the world from the end of the umbilical cord attached to us. Our job is knowing when to give them more cord and when to snap it taut.

Before I had a 2-year-old, I'd never have guessed this would be a time to begin that process or that I'd be able to participate.

A 2-year-old? Why, he was just born. Me let go? Why, I'm his mother.

Yet, somehow it happens. Babies turn into children who grow out and away. And we get to look on, growing, too, as they go.

Pregnancy is a community affair

June 20, 1991

When word got out that a co-worker was pregnant for the first time, I watched as mothers from throughout the office flocked to her desk.

They bombarded Dawn with stories of their own pregnancies, labors and deliveries. They railed on about the pioneer work that is yet to be done on behalf of working mothers and about how she needs to start looking for child care now.

I felt overwhelmed for my friend, who sat trapped while an office full of women hovered over her.

But then I skulked on over, too.

You can't help it. When you've had babies and then somebody else is having one, you've got to get your sticky little fingers on her.

The experienced mother (read: anybody who has a child) has got to pass along advice and wisdom, not to mention garbage bags full of faded maternity clothes and dog-eared copies of *What to Expect When You're Expecting*. She has to touch many a swelling belly, feel many a great kick and in the end, hang on the telling of many labor and delivery tales, which she will undoubtedly drown out with her own.

Living through somebody else's pregnancy allows the non-pregnant woman to experience the thrill of impending new life without the morning sickness and weight gain. It allows her to feel wise, like all that work wasn't for nothing if she can only pass it on.

Just this week, I was delighted to receive a long-distance call from another friend who's seven months' pregnant for the first time.

Anne could barely talk, she was so upset.

"I've been furious for a week and a half," she told me, her voice shaking.

I got goose bumps.

"My husband is always running around and wanting to have friends over. Half the time all I do is go home and go to bed."

I chuckled to myself, remembering.

"I think I'm really fighting this whole thing," Anne said. "I really resent being left behind, being told I'm not going to be able to do things that other people are doing."

I agreed with Anne, that, yes, hormones do make you crazy during pregnancy, that men do indeed seem to act more like men during pregnancy and that pregnancy can be very isolating.

My friend hung up feeling better.

I hung up feeling useful.

It's the same old conversation between women. But it's always new for women like Anne and Dawn who have never participated. And for those of us who have, these conversations allow us to relive the most special moments of our lives over and over and over.

That reliving is particularly poignant for those who don't plan on having those moments ever again.

As for others like me, as long as my maternity clothes and books are still out on loan, as long as I can hover and touch, advise and mother, I can pre-occupy my unmet urges a little while longer.

But not much longer.

When do parents get to sleep like babies?

Aug. 8, 1991

When my friend's 7-year-old daughter had to interview her mother for a homework assignment, she asked when she was born, where she was born and whether she enjoys her job. She also asked her mother to name her hobbies.

"Reading. Exercising. Sleeping," her mother replied.

Reading, now that's a popular leisure activity. Exercising, sure, a lot of people jog or do aerobics between work and home responsibilities.

But is my friend, a full-time professional who's dedicated to her husband, her church, two young children, a variety of friends and a rigorous exercise regime, so stretched that sleep has become something she does in her spare time?

Yes.

According to sleep experts, we Americans are experiencing a "national sleep deficit."

And nobody's more deficient than parents.

"We are one group of very tired people," said Helen Sullivan, a spokeswoman for the Better Sleep Council and a mother of two children under 6. "Here I am, I work for the Better Sleep Council, and I walk around with bags under my eyes."

The reason is simple. Newborns like to eat, so they wake up. They wake up every couple of hours for a long time. A long time. If they have colic, they might not sleep at all. When infants are awake, somebody must tend them, even if that somebody could really use the sleep. Children 1 to 3 don't always sleep through the night, either, for reasons that include fear of separation, fear of bed-wetting, fear of fear itself and just because. From 4 to 6, once-, twice-, even thrice-nightly waking can be the result of bed-wetting, sleepwalking and night terrors. Same with 6 to 12. Of course, when children are awake, so is everybody else in the house.

You can do your best to get used to your child's sleep interruptions. You can resolve to keep your eyes closed as you're getting the baby back to sleep so you will have less trouble doing the same for yourself. You can catch up on sleep by taking naps on the weekends when the youngest children do, unplugging the phone and threatening to dismantle the tricycle of any family member who disturbs you. You can even learn to relish night wakings, as one single working father of three claimed he learned to do.

"I looked forward to the middle-of-the-night ritual of walking the baby, singing him songs and feeling him fall asleep at my neck, only then to have David wake up, needing a change, a bottle, walking or singing," William Van Hert wrote in his collection of essays, *Being a Father.*

Surely, such blissful parenting before the rooster crows is rare. The parents with whom I'm more familiar will try any trick in the book to get that baby to sleep.

There's the pacifier trick recommended by the Better Sleep Council. This one is supposed to work on babies who can't go to sleep without a pacifier but then drop it throughout the night and yell for you to come get it. The council says the parent should just throw a hundred pacifiers in the crib before the baby goes to bed. Every time a pacifier falls, the baby can reach out and find another. At more than $2 a pacifier, that's some investment. But what if it works?

There's the "Let them cry it out" method. This is for parents of young children who seem only to want their presence. After a few nights, the kid gets the message that Mom and Dad aren't coming and quits crying, says sleep expert Richard Ferber who explains this method step-by-step in his highly acclaimed book, *Solve Your Child's Sleep Problem.* Some parents think Ferber's technique cruel. But what if it works?

The most reasoned method for getting a child to enjoy a blissful sleep involves no tricks at all. Establishing a nighttime routine—a warm bath before bed, reading books together and an early bedtime—and presto, you might not hear anything until the alarm clock rings

As for coping with sleep deprivation when you can't figure out a way to get it, the Sleep Council suggests that parents let the housework go and go to bed as soon as the baby does. Make sleep a priority.

And when all else fails, I say stifle that yawn, put some Wite-Out on those bags under your eyes and imagine that far-off time when you're lonely for the sounds of a child crying in the night.

When the women run away

Aug. 29, 1991

We were seven women, all of us wives, most of us mothers, most of us full-time employees. We were, without exception, needing to get away.

And so we did, many of us for the first time in years without spouse, work and/or child. We drove to a campground three hours from home. We put up four sleep tents and a screened tent by ourselves. We ate. We drank. We hiked 3.2 miles to the top of a mountain and 3.2 miles down.

We hung out, so loudly one night that a campground manager had to warn us to be quiet. We whispered and giggled like guilty Girl Scouts when he turned on his heel, the beam of his big flashlight bouncing away with great authority.

More than anything we talked.

We couldn't stop talking.

Some of us brought books. Some of us had plans to take long naps on our long weekend. Instead, we sat around the screened tent and the picnic tables talking common ground. It wasn't hard to find, despite the difference in age and persuasion, hairstyles and bad habits, despite the fact that some of us had never met before. Well into the night, you could hear whispers from individual tents.

We talked about how lucky we are to have good husbands and about how we shouldn't have to say we're lucky. But we're lucky nonetheless because our husbands "let" us leave them with the responsibilities while we went away to have none.

We talked about our children. Of course, we talked about our children, about whether and when we can fit more of them into our lives. We talked about how we feed, discipline and love, and some of us realized with some dismay that such discussion meant we had officially become our mothers.

We talked about them collectively, our husbands and our children, our families, and how hard it is to make it all come together these days. How, as enlightened as we think we are, we still have to help our husbands understand that we're different from their mothers. That we can't do everything anymore. Those of us with male children realized we are responsible for teaching them not to expect too much of the women in their lives.

We talked jobs and stress. We tried not to talk too much jobs and stress.

The air was full of excitement that weekend, despite the quiet in the mountains where we camped.

It wasn't like we'd never talked to other women about these things or hiked up a mountain or put up a tent.

But until you get in a group where everybody is saying the same things, you never really know whether your best friend has been telling you all this time that you're OK because she's your best friend.

And until you leave your commitments for the first time, you're never sure whether you can or not. You're never sure all your responsibilities will let you. Or that you will let yourself.

In the real world, everything is on a time line. Everybody has a need, and when you're a woman, it seems somebody is needing you every minute. Women can lose themselves in our kind of world.

We seemed to realize in that small space and time that we didn't want that happening to us and, perhaps more importantly, that it didn't have to happen to us.

They lived without us that weekend, all of them, the husbands, the children and the bosses.

I'm convinced that my child ate nothing but potato chips and pizza. The house seemed dirtier. But everybody lived without me. And my husband was proud of himself, and of me, for doing what I'd been threatening to do and what he'd been encouraging me to do for a long time.

I was glad to be back with my family. I was also glad to find out that if I ever need to pull myself away again, I can.

Not only that, I must.

The dreaded diaper deadline

Sept. 12, 1991

We encountered last weekend the potential for a royal event.

His highness removed his diaper. He ascended the porcelain throne. He seated himself. And looking into the face of his loyal subject, he said:

"Mommy, I need another diaper."

Then he jumped down and wandered away, leaving me to wonder what I did wrong this time.

I never understood all the fuss before. I refused to buy into Freudian repression theories; the idea that toilet training too late or too early means forever lost opportunities; or the notion that the way you teach a child to control his bodily functions will define your parenting skills forevermore.

I hadn't cared about the hype but had planned only to be a conduit in a little person's search for independence and good riddance to sticky plastic on his bottom. I was going to show him where to do it and how to do it and let him figure out the rest.

But every day, the magic, last-chance-for-continence age of 3 looms closer.

Every day, more of his playmates leave him in the baby-powder dust on the changing table as they join the ranks of the sure and dry.

Likewise, my peers, the same ones who used to huddle together reminding each other that you don't see 18-year-olds wearing diapers, are becoming fewer and fewer.

And so, buckling under potty peer pressure, I've been skulking out of the library again with the same potty picture books I skulked out with six months ago. I've been doling out the Gummi Bear bribes I said I'd never give. I've been doing what everybody else does: I've been giving entirely too much attention to one developmental milestone.

We have our ancestors to thank for this obsession. In the early 20th century, babies were held over chamber pots before they could sit up. By the time they were 10 months old, it was routine to be held over the potty on the hour. Ultimately, the baby was strapped in and made to sit for long periods of time until something happened.

It was a rigorous schedule to keep up, particularly since such rigors rarely produced potty-trained children. But mothers were desperate to get out from under all those hand-washed diapers. They also were spurred on by a theory that toilet training isn't just a way to keep a child dry; toileting also provides the child with that famous sense of order.

Thank goodness today's parenting gurus no longer promote such rigid methods. Parenting manuals these days encourage parents to watch the child for clues that he's ready, including an ability to keep a diaper dry more than two hours and an awareness that something is about to come out of his body.

Still, we're left with the potty training legends, not the least of which is perpetrated by our own imperious mothers. To hear them tell it, we were potty-trained before we could sit up.

My husband and I have taken Christopher to the store and ceremoniously picked out a special little potty.

The potty sits full of dust in a corner of the bathroom.

We have presented him with colorful packs of underwear. Twice.

We have pointed out the fact that the mailman, the policeman, the garbage man and the doctor all go potty.

All to no avail, all of which should tell us to back off, to let him make his own way.

But the ghosts of toilet order keep after us.

And all the while, the king of the bathroom, who is enjoying a battle of wills he so obviously is winning, is eagerly eyeing the next sized Pampers in the grocery store.

Happy birthday to you—but what's your theme?

Sept. 26, 1991

When I was growing up, a birthday party meant family members gathered in the back yard and sang "Happy Birthday." The birthday boy or girl opened a pile of inexpensive presents and then dumped his or her face in the cake.

It was cheap and simple family fun, which my husband and I tried duplicating last year for our child's second birthday. Only thing, my husband and I were the only guests, since we're Christopher's only in-town family members.

Christopher stood on a chair and looked at the balloons suspended from the dining room chandelier. He opened four presents. We decided not to have a cake because we'd already taken cupcakes to child care that morning.

And two minutes after the party started, the birthday boy toddled off to another part of the house while my husband and I sat in the middle of the wrapping paper and said, "Now what?"

This year we decided to broaden our horizons.

"We're going to have a birthday bash for Christopher and his friends," I announced to the mother of a 3-year-old and a 6-year-old.

"What's your theme?" my friend asked.

"Theme?"

"You know, the idea that makes your event hold together."

"I thought it was the fact that Christopher is turning 3," I said.

"No, no, no. What kind of sports does he like?"

"Baseball, I think," I said.

"Great. I know a baker who can make a baseball cake."

"I was thinking Christopher and I would make his cake together."

"Don't go to the trouble. This baker can make the cake look like a baseball. Then you can have baseball hats and balls for party favors."

"Party favors?"

"You have to have party favors," she said, by now impatient with such naivete. "They expect party favors."

It has become clear that they expect this annually, too. In my continuing determination to understand modern-day childhood, I have discovered 10-year-olds who have never missed having a birthday party with all their friends. Even for first birthday parties, parents invite all the other babies from child care.

Birthday bashes have become so competitive that a recent issue of a popular parenting magazine included a 50-page guide to throwing "the best birthday bashes ever, including foolproof birthday cakes and perfect party favors, tips on games, videotaping and ideas for decorations." Headings include "Plan the best birthday ever!" "Coping with party payback," "Whom to invite?" and "At home or away?"

One mother wouldn't even tell me the theme of her 6-year-old daughter's upcoming party because she didn't want her friends to steal it.

As a former birthday girl whose simplest pleasure was licking the icing off the candles, I thought this an awful lot of indulgence for a child, a byproduct of the overdone loss-of-extended-family-parental-guilt-because-of-working syndrome. At first. I bucked. At first.

But it's hard not to indulge when everybody else is, especially when there's a child involved.

Especially when it's your child.

I'm still not going all out for Christopher's birthday this year. I'm not going to entertain the kids or set up elaborate games. I'm still making the cake.

But I will establish a "theme" with a Big Bird tablecloth and some hats if that's what they want. I'll put bubbles and bouncy balls in brown paper bags and pass them out as party favors.

I'll strike a happy medium between a 90-second yawner like his second birthday party and a dog-and-pony show, although I've conceded that a dog and a pony could very well show up for some future celebration.

It is, after all, my child's birth day.

Through a child's eyes

Nov. 21, 1991

They warn you when you're preparing to have your first child how you'll be forced to change thousands of diapers and your life. How you'll struggle to find child care and sleep. How you'll never have enough money, time or inclination to do anything for yourself ever again.

What they forget to tell you is how you will feel when you take your very own child to the circus, where he gets so delirious he screams instead of laughs.

Or what it will be like to help your child dress for his first Halloween party and then watch as he discovers his playmates have become pirates and cowboys, ballerinas and princesses.

Left to your own devices, though, you quickly discover that simply listening is a treat. When a car pulled out in front of me the other day and I had to slam on the brakes, my 3-year-old said, "Dammit, dammit, dammit." Oops.

There was another time in the car when he was singing to himself and looking out the window, smiling.

I said, "You seem so happy today. Are you happy?"

He shook his head yes.

I said, "What makes you happy?"

"Love," he said.

I laughed and laughed, and he did, too.

They tell you secrets.

"Candy is my favorite food," he told me the other day.

No kidding.

They say things to other people that might be embarrassing, except that it's a child saying them.

"Are you a rabbit?" he asked an elderly neighbor whose rain hat most certainly was sticking up on top.

You and your child begin to develop favorite conversations, like the one about when he was born. And what mother doesn't delight in reliving that occasion over and over?

My child provides me constant companionship. On the weekends, if there's a drive to be made or an airplane to point out in the sky, if there's a whale on TV or a festival in town, you can bet he will want to see.

He is easy to please, much easier than any adult. He oohs and aahs over a marching band and doesn't even notice there's no football game. He likes going to the park and seeing what color the leaves are. He likes going to a parade and pointing to an American flag. He likes watching *Bambi* on the VCR and pealing with laughter when Thumper does.

Watching him has helped me recall the world from a child's point of view, even when I'm not with him.

Alone in the car the other day, I saw a cow on the side of the road. "Look!" I started to alert Christopher. By the time I remembered he wasn't in the car with me, it was too late. I had already been excited simply to see a cow.

I remember to look for full moons now. Last night, we saw an airplane fly across one. I see birds on the feeder and children in the park. I see firefighters washing bright, red fire engines and garbage collectors driving big, blue trucks.

These are the things I would forget to see if I didn't have a child. These are the things I would forget to hear, fail to experience.

These are the things that the experienced among us forget to tell the uninitiated as they prepare to head into this heady experience called parenthood.

Perhaps we don't tell each other because it sounds too hokey—the idea that you can actually rediscover childhood.

Perhaps we don't tell each other because we don't want to boast.

But it's true, what they say: Children do change your life.

When second thoughts turn to action

Dec. 26, 1991

I wanted to be pregnant with my second child as soon as I quit being pregnant with my first.

I missed the intimacy associated with hiding a child under my skirts for nine months. I missed the anticipation. I missed my Breyer's vanilla every night.

I was the only one in the house who felt this way.

My husband, who spent the first pregnancy in shock, spent the next three years thinking up reasons why we shouldn't do it again just yet.

He reasoned. I waited. Until finally one day he acknowledged that ovaries probably don't produce eggs forever. And we began meeting for intimate "lunches" at home during a certain key time of the month.

Our lunches took. Now, whether his arguments about not enough money, patience or rooms in the house were applicable, they are finally moot–as are any notions I had about a second pregnancy being just like the first.

Unlike my first pregnancy, my head is not in the clouds this time because it's closer to the toilet.

The special attention is not so pervasive this time. The mothers who hover so closely over first pregnancies don't bother as much with a second-timer.

I'm worried more this time, perhaps because this time I'm branded "over 35."

This time is different for another reason.

This reason tells people, "I'm going to be a brother."

He holds his arms up for me to pick him but not before he says, "I promise I won't hurt the baby."

He pulls up my shirt and asks, "Is your tummy bigger?"

We've been preparing our 3-year-old son for the event that will take place five months from now. Just as my husband and I talked and talked with each other about the one-day occurrence of a second child, so had we talked to Christopher. We took him to see our friends' newborn babies and purposely left the crib up in his room, telling him a new baby might sleep in it one day.

Little does Christopher know, though, that one baby means he's king. Two babies means he shares his room, his toys and his mommy and daddy.

Just as his parents could never anticipate the joys and trials that two babies will bring our family, neither can he know until it happens the concept of being a big brother.

Regardless, he is excited.

We all are. And it is that unanimous excitement that has made the wait, the wading through the excuses until we were both ready, worth it.

This time, WE are going to have a baby.

Don't call me names

Jan. 9, 1992

My son has told me to quit calling him darling.

I'm also not to call him pumpkin pie, love muffin or lamb.

I'm only to call him boy.

"Hey, boy," I'm supposed to say when I greet my 3-year-old.

That is, unless I'm calling him by his real name. Then I'm to call him Chris. Not Christopher.

I'm not surprised at this demonstration. He's been wiping my kisses away for quite awhile now.

But I will miss Christopher, since I think it's the prettier of the two names and since it took my husband and me most of my pregnancy, plus 48 hours, to settle on it.

There's a lot in a name, after all. It defines a child and the way people think about him. A Susan always and forever more acts like a Susan, an Audrey an Audrey. John is always John, Kim is Kim and George is just that.

We didn't want our child's name to be either too cute or too plain. My husband didn't want a one-syllable first name against a one-syllable last name. We didn't want to name the child after a grandparent on one side and not the other.

Somehow, we clicked early in pregnancy on a girl's name. We agreed on the poetic Savannah, a name we discovered in Pat Conroy's Southern novel, *The Prince of Tides*.

As for a boy's name, my husband was determined all the way to the time of his birth, and later, that any boy of ours would be named Russell, a popular Hook family name. I was determined all the way to the time of his birth, and later, that no boy of ours would be named Russell, since the only Russell I ever knew was a guy I once dated who turned out to be a jerk. Not only that, but Rusty Hook?

And so, the morning after Russell-to-be-or-not-to-be was born, the doctor came in. What's his name, the doctor asked, medical pen poised over medical chart. We had nothing to say.

The people with the birth certificate came. Twice.

We tried various boy names with various connotations during Christopher's first 48 hours. He was Dylan for a few minutes because we went to a Bob Dylan concert in my ninth month of pregnancy. He was Dustin for a few hours because we both like Dustin Hoffman. We tried Russell again, but I couldn't get past that bad relationship.

Somehow, we mutually landed on the melodic Christopher. It had that poetic sound to it. It happened to be the name of a close friend who died young. We rolled the name over our tongues.

"Christopher! It's supper time!" "Christopher! Clean up this room!" "Christopher Hook, *magna cum laude.*"

Other than making a baby, it was the most significant thing my husband and I had done together in a long time. We loved the name we picked.

And now he doesn't. I guess he thinks Christopher sounds like a baby's name.

Now he's Chris Hook. Chris Hook. The name moves so fast, just like his life has. Once a darling, now a boy. Once kissable, now untouchable.

It's OK. I predicted he'd one day choose the more grown-up Chris. My mother watched as I changed from Debra, to Debbie, now Debra-Lynn. I suppose he should have that choice, too.

It's his life, after all.

And this is just the beginning, only the first of many times we'll proudly present him with something, only to have him make it into something of his own.

Envy and the pregnant body builder

Jan. 23, 1991

One of the best things about pregnancy is not having to hold your stomach in anymore.

One of the worst is pregnancy underwear: One size fits hips 30 inches to 52 inches. In the early stages of pregnancy, there's so much material, the waistband covers your chest. In the end, the overstretched cotton barely stretches to cover what used to be your belly button. Such appealing apparel they make for mothers-to-be.

The other worst thing is picture-perfect pregnant people like Penny Price, a bodybuilder and cover model for national muscle magazines who's supposed to have her first child in three weeks.

I say "supposed to." Based on normal pregnant people standards, Price, 32, doesn't look or act like she's going to have anything. Through almost nine months of pregnancy, Price has gained 12 pounds.

Forgive me while I pout into my pickles and ice cream. Her weight gain is little more than what the average non-pregnant person gains during several weeks of Christmas indulgence. Her "worst thing" of pregnancy is her little bump of a stomach poking into the clients she coaches at the gym where she works. Her workout capability is equally disgusting.

"I usually work out five days a week for about an hour and a half," she told me by phone from her home in Altamonte Springs, Fla. "I do a split body workout, all with weight training—chest, shoulders, triceps one day, then legs, back and biceps the second day. Since I've been pregnant, I've lightened up on the weights, not a great deal, just on things that are more full body workouts, like squats. I do them only once every two weeks. Normally I could squat 150 pounds. Now I do 95 pounds."

Not only that, but: "Five days a week I power-walk 2 to 6 miles a day," Price said.

On one hand, I'm envious. On the other hand, I have to wonder if what Price is doing is healthy for her or the baby.

Price thinks she's doing the right thing. Price says women have been wrongly conditioned to believe they have to lose control of their bodies, i.e., get fat, when they get pregnant.

"A majority of women I see gain 30 to 50 pounds," Price said. "I think a real reason for that is lack of control. Even after the third month, my appetite was going crazy. I kept catching myself saying 'I'm pregnant, I'm allowed to gain weight.' That's how all these women gain weight. It's a great excuse."

Sounds like the propaganda of the 1950s, if you ask me, when women were put on salad diets if they gained more than 15 or 20 pounds. Of course, having gained in 4½ months what Price gained in nine, I have my own agenda.

But if you listen to the academic wisdom of the '90s, I'm on the wiser track. While OBs in the 1950s kept mama's weight down to keep baby's weight down to make deliveries easier, they now know to a certain point that a heavier mama is a heavier baby is a healthier baby. OBs and midwives now advise women to gain 25 to 30, up to 35 and 40, pounds during pregnancy.

Does that mean Price and other women who choose such a regimen are destined to have unhealthy babies?

Price's midwife, Mary Ann Becker, who said she's seeing an increasing number of fat-conscious, exercise-conscious women in her practice, said she once delivered a 10-pound baby to a woman who gained 15 pounds during pregnancy.

"I believe that in the state of pregnancy everything goes to the baby first," Becker said. "You'd have to have a mom in pretty extreme malnutrition before it influences the baby, because the baby is going to live off the stores on the mother's body.

"In Penny's case, where she's eating plenty, I think most of it goes to the baby, and because of the workouts, she burns the rest of it off.

"As far as her matching up to other pregnancies, with uterine growth and blood testing, she's doing fine," Becker said. "She looks small when she stands there, but she falls well within the parameters for uterine growth."

Yet, even though she feels confident about the baby's outcome, Becker is not so sure that Price's regime won't cause her problems in other ways. A lot of the fat a woman stores during pregnancy is pulled on later for breast feeding. Price won't have those stores.

Also, Becker said, she's heard of athletes with placentas that don't want to come out because their perineal muscles are so strong. Once Becker tried unsuccessfully to turn a breech baby that she's convinced wouldn't turn because the mother's abdominal muscles were too strong to let go.

Becker said Price, who relied on instincts with regard to her body, might end up being some kind of test case in a world of research that is just now beginning to realize pregnant women want to exercise, too, sometimes vigorously.

"Really, the last time the American College of Obstetricians and Gynecologists said they were going to put out a statement and an exercise film, it was the kind of thing where they said 'Raise one arm, then raise the other arm.' People who were into exercise said 'That's silly.' We need some good research."

I guess we'll have to wait and see what happens with Price.

In the meanwhile, I'm going to continue to envy people like her, but only to a point.

She's not going to have nearly the battle with extra weight postpartum that I am. And I bet she never filled out her maternity underwear.

But pregnancy is about the only time in my life when I allow myself to slip a little. To eat a teeny little bowl of ice cream every night. To slow down on aerobics. To relax: For once in my life, the fat on my thighs has a purpose.

(P.S. I followed up with Price after she had her baby. She had a four-hour delivery with no complications and a 7-pound, 11-ounce baby boy. She had no problems breast feeding for five months. The day after she delivered, she weighed four pounds less than the day she got pregnant. By the time she was four months postpartum, she had her body back the way it was before she got pregnant. At nine months postpartum, she participated in and placed fifth in a national body-building contest. Well.)

It's the little things

Feb. 20, 1992

Imagine the size of the plastic shoes that go on the feet of a 2-inch-tall toy clown.

Imagine Fisher-Price people and animals no bigger than your thumb, centimeter-sized LEGO blocks, bits of crayons and chalk, Discovery cups and chain links and hundreds of minuscule, miscellaneous items that appear to have no purpose.

These are the little things that pile up in a house where little children live. These are the things parents are accustomed to finding, in the bathtub, in the purse, under the couch, under the bed, under the covers when they go to bed at night, in multiples on the floor of a child's room minutes after it's been cleaned.

After many months of watching such items accumulate and wondering how many more our house could handle, I finally started saving the rectangular containers that baby wipes come in.

Little people go in one, animals go in another, blocks go in another, miscellaneous in another.

I have found great joy in these containers.

Indeed, I have found few things more gratifying than helping a little boy clean up his room and watching him discover that he has a home for all his things.

Nothing is more rewarding for the relentless parent—unless it's finding the shoes that belong to the clown, who's been barefoot since he came home from the store.

A house where little children live is full of other little things—tiny clothes, for example.

A dryer only half-full of clothes to be folded actually is 15 pairs of pants, 15 shirts and 15 pairs of socks. The socks are so tiny they tend to slip through the crack between the agitator and the bottom of the washing machine and stop it up.

Open the refrigerator of the young child's home and you will find small containers of yogurt and apple sauce, half-eaten. They are bits of food that might not seem worth saving, but they actually are a plentiful snack for a little stomach waiting for dinner.

Open a dresser drawer and you will find nail scissors so tiny and so tender they could be used to cut the nails of a doll's hand.

In a house where little children live are nooks and crannies too small to hide an adult during hide and seek, but just the right size for a little playmate.

In a house where little children live are little books. They are no bigger than the palm of an adult hand, but they fit quite nicely between the palms of their owner.

The home of a young child inevitably includes a menagerie of tiny stuffed animals given at birth and birthdays. A parent might consider packing away or giving away at least some of them until one afternoon when a creative little mind uses them to make a zoo.

The parent of the young child learns to find a place for these and all the other irritating little things that collect in the little person's house.

It would be very easy to rake much of it into a pile and sneak it to the trash. We big people have that kind of control.

But of all the containers in my young boy's room, the one he goes to most is the one set aside for the miscellaneous items. Inside are the items that have no meaning to me. But he knows what to do with them. He knows what they mean.

We can throw away the things that are meaningless to us. Or we can realize they're not meaningless to a child.

We can give little feelings little attention. Or we can realize that children have needs that won't wait.

We can shuffle little children and little things to the side. Or we can realize that just because a child's world is smaller than ours doesn't mean it's any less important.

We can realize little people especially need big people they can trust to understand these little things.

Pamper me, please

March 26, 1992

Some people get cranky when they get pregnant.

I get speeding tickets.

I'm not sure why. It could be that I always drive fast and that I just happened to get caught twice during my first pregnancy and twice during this one.

It could also be that I drive faster when I'm pregnant. I figure if I get pulled over, the officer will acquiesce to my protruding stomach.

Other people do. Other people jump up to give up the last chair in the room to the waddling woman holding her lower back, refuse to let her carry heavy things and otherwise pander to women with babies in their bellies.

This can go to extremes, depending on the generation and gender of the person. A middle-aged man seeing a pregnant woman carrying the tiniest of parcels will insist that you not do that.

Oftentimes people will call attention to your pregnancy when it has nothing to do with your relationship with them.

When my car broke down out of town a few weeks ago—cars and I apparently don't get along when I'm gestating—the mechanic with whom I was discussing electrical wiring suddenly blurted out, "You don't want your car to break down on the road in YOUR CONDITION."

I love this attention. And I hate it.

For the first few months, I can't wait for it. I stick out my pelvis and I put my hands on my hips to make my stomach as obvious as possible.

Then, when my belly finally does speak for itself, I want people to acknowledge my pregnancy. But only when I want them to.

I want the attention when I'm in the mood to be mothered myself—or I'm trying to influence a police officer.

I don't want it when I'm trying to be professional or when I'm standing in the Sears Auto Shop with half a dozen men.

I likewise would prefer to go unnoticed in exercise class, where the demographic is working women in color-coordinated outfits who mean business when they take a lunch hour to exercise.

Trying to fit in with the crowd at seven months pregnant, I wanted to hide under my over-sized T-shirt recently when the instructor stared at me and boomed into the microphone, "If you're pregnant, you need to check your pulse periodically."

Unfortunately, you can't always tell people when they should pay attention to your pregnant self, and when they should overlook you. People see a pregnant woman coming, and they see pregnant. You have to take the attention as it comes—and sometimes as it doesn't.

I remember how disappointed I was one day when the attention didn't come.

It was me and cars again. It was four years ago, and I was in labor. I couldn't find my husband. And so I had to drive myself to the hospital.

I recall no greater joy from that day—with perhaps the exception of giving birth—than running every red light there was between home and the hospital and hoping for once that a police officer would pull me over so I could do my Lamaze breathing for him.

Unfortunately, you can't pick and choose when the speed police will be lurking, any more than you can pick when a stranger is going to offer to carry a heavy package for you and when you're going to have to carry it yourself.

A friend who is due to have her first baby in a couple of months was commiserating with me recently, wondering why is it that the same people ask her every other day, "Now when is it that you're due?"

I get tired of it, too. But I also wonder what life as a pregnant woman would be like if nobody noticed me.

I don't think we can have it both ways. And so I guess I have to say, bring on that overt attention—unless it's in the form of a traffic ticket. It'll all be gone soon enough.

Second baby's on the way . . . But where to put the first?

May 7, 1992

The crib is up. The baby clothes are washed and sorted. I feel prepared for the coming of a second child.

Now if I could only get the first one out of our bed.

It would be one thing if my husband and I had been inviting 3-year-old Christopher to crawl out of his bed and into ours in the middle of the night.

But while some parents have made an institution of the "family bed," my husband and I didn't commit to this by conscious choice.

No, I sheepishly admit this nightly routine was made so in our family by semi-conscious parents who simply found it easier to move over than to get up.

I've tried to reason with Christopher, gently reminding him that big boys sleep alone in their own beds.

"But Mommy and Daddy don't sleep alone," is his rightful reply, to which I have none.

I've already tried all the tricks, including the subliminal approach, whispering to him as he falls asleep in his own bed, "Sleep through the night. Please." He always mumbles OK. But there he always appears a few hours later, standing at my side of the bed and asking to climb in.

This can be sweet. Like when a little voice says in the middle of the night, "I love you, Mommy." Or when I wake to see an angel's face next to mine on the pillow.

It's sweet for him, too. "We're all together," he says happily, as he falls back to sleep.

Of course, other things are sweet in la-la land, too, such as:

Uninterrupted sleep.

Privacy.

Not fighting at 4 a.m. for the pillow with the flowers.

Rolling over.

And now that we've got a fourth family member on the way, I'm thinking I should practice crowd control before we have one in our bed.

At least we're not alone. A recent issue of *Parenting* says the majority of parents at least occasionally allow small children to crawl into bed with them. Most of them, unsure that what they're doing is a good idea, make half-hearted attempts to send the tyke back to the hallows of his room.

One couple sounded just like us, determined during the day to put their 18-month-old son in his place. Then night would come.

"When 3 o'clock rolled around and he wandered in, we ended up just doing whatever would get us all back to sleep the fastest—in other words, letting him come in with us," said Sharon Tehan of Watertown, Mass. "We just didn't have the energy to put him back in bed. We'd say 'Forget it, we'll try it tomorrow.' "

At 4, Tehan's child still tries to sleep with his parents. But he's too big to fit in the bed now. And so one of his parents has resorted to lying down in his bed with him until he falls asleep, while the other parent stares up at the ceiling from the marital bed.

Child development experts differ on this topic. Some say the family bed delays independence, fostering a sense that the child is not a separate person. Children don't learn that the marriage bed is a special place, they say.

Wisdom on the other hand says co-sleeping is better than the alternative for babies and young children who like to be cuddled. Rather than having to undergo the trauma of learning to sleep alone, they get to slumber peacefully surrounded by love and security. It's mostly in western industrial societies, and only over the past century, that separating babies and small children from their mothers' beds has become the norm.

I happen to be one who doesn't think there's anything particularly wrong with sleeping with young children. I think stages of independence come when they come. If I don't do anything active to get Christopher out of our bed, one day soon he'll do it himself.

What I think it comes down to is parental choice. And if the whole family, including the parents, likes the family bed, then family bed it is.

If, on the other hand, they are more uncomfortable with co-sleeping than comfortable, then they should use firm, consistent measures to stop it. Soon enough, they will find themselves with a child who has forgotten all about those warm nights of youth when they curled up safe and warm against Mommy or Daddy. The family against the world. Everybody together.

Kids are resilient, so they say. They'll get over it.

The question is: Will you?

Babies deserve the truth about themselves

May 21, 1992

If you ask this pregnant mother, society has fallen short with its latest attempt at sex education, the invention of a mommy doll with a removable stomach wall and a baby inside.

To the manufacturer's credit, the doll indicates we're becoming increasingly realistic about our responsibility to teach children where babies really come from.

But the doll tells only half the truth. Babies don't come out of stomachs, as a rule.

Of course, that's what I told my 3-year-old when I found out I was pregnant again.

Having grown up with parents who thought sex education was handing their children a book at age 12, I didn't consider telling him anything but "There's a baby in Mommy's tummy."

Then I met a mother of two who had told her 3-year-old a different story when she was pregnant. She told her child that a baby was growing in her uterus and that her baby was going to come out of her vagina. She even showed her preschooler vivid, close-up photographs of a baby being born.

I was shocked at first by her candid approach. But as my pregnancy progressed, and I continued to endure the persistent inquisition of a child watching his mommy's "tummy" grow, I began to wonder how not to tell my son the truth. And why not.

Sex educators know this isn't easy stuff for parents. As children, most of us were told tales of storks and cabbage patches until we were old enough to have a book about puberty thrust at our budding adolescence—if we were that lucky.

It was ingrained in many of us that children aren't sexual beings until they're old enough to get those books and that parents don't discuss sex with them until then.

"Parents, adults, are very concerned about protecting children," said Trish Moylan Torruella, director of education at Planned Parenthood Federation of America. "It's OK for kids to understand if they're boys or girls, but the erotic aspects we're afraid of. We think if we give them the reality, we're endangering them."

In fact, as sex education consultant Lynn Leight explains in *Raising Sexually Healthy Children*, children are sexual beings before they're born; boys get erections in the womb. As early as 18 months, children begin locating body parts. At age 3, they express curiosity about the differences between boys and girls. When they're 6, they play doctor. From 7 to 9, they giggle, tell dirty jokes and become self-conscious about approaching body changes. And so on.

In short, children are sexual beings always, and they begin showing curiosity and awareness about that aspect of themselves early on, just like everything else in their world.

By talking casually about sexuality with children as early in their lives as possible, we offset the mystique, the shame and confusion that comes from learning half-truths from peers and halfway appropriate dolls. We open up lines of communication that don't have to be opened up later.

By starting early and continuing to talk with our children, we start them out with a healthy view of sexuality, as a "natural, healthy, and wonderful part of life that can have some negative consequences if we are irresponsible or uninformed about the choices," Torruella said.

I don't know that I considered any of this when I started telling my young son the truth. It's just that he was asking the questions. I simply had to figure out a way to answer them.

I even showed him some of those vivid photographs. There was no "Ewyukky, Mommy" like I feared there might be. I don't think he even knew he was supposed to be disgusted or embarrassed. He listened to what I was telling him like I was telling him that apples grow on trees and planes fly in the sky.

Once I discovered how comfortable he was with our discussions, I began to feel comfortable, too. I even began to look for opportunities to tell him more than he bargained for.

This is still new. I still have to battle my own embarrassment even as my son displays none. Somehow, I keep skipping right over the part about how Mommy and Daddy actually made that baby inside me.

But I'll get to it. I will.

I know now, as I try not to blush when I talk with my son, that hearing the truth when I was young and curious would have served me better, too.

Gender games

June 4, 1992

I am bemused by people who think they can take one look at my bulging belly and know whether I'm having a boy or a girl.

I'd like to know how they know. Because my husband and I don't.

This must put us in a minority. Whereas a generation ago, most pregnant women didn't have access to such knowledge, today's medical technology now makes it easy to learn the sex of an unborn child. Whereas the question "Do you know what you're having?" never would have been asked a generation ago, it's one of the first questions asked of pregnant women today.

I guess to some ways of thinking the parents-to-be are better off knowing. Knowing the baby's gender means they won't waste time picking two names. If they know whether they're going to have a boy or a girl, they can stock up on gender-specific baby clothes before the baby is born. Maybe parents who desperately want one sex or the other think they will be better prepared in the birth room if they know the sex of their child beforehand.

To my way of thinking, few things are sacred anymore.

If I didn't have the gender of the child to dream about during pregnancy, labor and delivery, I'm afraid I'd focus on all the things that could go wrong. This way, there's a surprise to look forward to, a twist at the end.

Keeping gender a mystery makes the end result more fun for family and friends, too. Hearing me announce "I had a girl! I had a boy!" has got to be more exciting than "I had a baby!" They already knew I was going to do that.

Keeping gender a mystery also keeps the guessing games going. Unfounded as I think the predicating is, it's fun. It also diverts my attention from fatigue, indigestion and the incessant wait for the due date. Some of the games can get quite elaborate. All are played out with great seriousness, to include:

• How You're Carrying. This must be the one people use when they make those quick once-overs of my belly. According to this one, if the woman is carrying the baby low and like a football, it's a boy. If she's carrying high and wide, girl.

• Wedding Ring on a String. The pregnant woman ties her wedding ring to a string, then lies flat on her back and has someone suspend the ring over her stomach. If it rotates counterclockwise, it's a boy. Clockwise, it's a girl.

• Squeezed Chin. The pregnant woman gets somebody to squeeze the fatty part of her chin. If it creases in the middle, it's a girl. If it doesn't, it's a boy.

• Slow-Fast Heartbeat. Slow fetal heartbeat, as determined during monthly prenatal visits, is a boy. Fast is a girl.

• Different Pregnancy. A woman whose second pregnancy is dramatically different than the first is having a different gender than she had the first time.

• 60/40. If the mother thinks she's having one gender, there's a 60 percent chance she's having the other.

Based on the results of these games, I'm having boy, girl, boy, boy, girl, girl, respectively.

I think that about evens out the odds.

All of which boils down to: Nobody knows, although whoever predicts the winning gender will be even more convinced their method of prediction works.

Not knowing keeps this sense of play in the air. What else have I got to do?

Not knowing also keeps me open-minded. I can think about wanting a girl because I've never had one. I can think about wanting a boy because my 3½-year-old son would like a little brother.

Not knowing takes the seriousness off gender and puts it on what I know I want, for sure:

A child, boy or girl, as healthy as the first one.

A child, boy or girl, as lovable as the first one.

A child, boy or girl, soon, please.

Babies

Oct. 8, 1992

Just like my second pregnancy, I had expectations for my second experience with birth and new life. I expected it to be different.

Right away, it was.

I had a girl this time, someone to equal out the gender balance in our family, someone to give my husband and me the pleasure of saying, "We have one of each," someone to dress in the now-faded pink dresses my mother saved for me. For a girl I will consider mother/daughter relationships from a brand-new perspective. I will cherish the poetry of her feminine name, Emily.

Emily is different from my firstborn in other ways. She is petite where he is burly. She is turning dark-eyed already at 3 months where his 4-year-old eyes are green. I had expected physical differences, and yet I'm still awed that a set of genes can be so distinct as to give her two clearly visible dimples in her cheeks when nobody else in our family has much of one.

Giving birth to her was different, as I'd expected. Whereas the first time I didn't think I had choices, this time I sought them out. This time a midwife helped me deliver my child as the summer sun streaked through the blinds of our bedroom window.

There are other fundamental differences. This baby eats small meals. The other couldn't get enough. This baby slept through the night early on. The first one still doesn't.

Whereas my first baby had no competition, my second baby has had to wait her turn. But the second also has had the joy of watching an elfin creature flit in and out of her line of vision, hugging her, kissing her, begging to carry her and matter-of-factly telling one friend who had held her too long: "That's our baby. Give her back."

They tell you it will be different. Those who have gone before you tell you no two babies or birth experiences are alike and neither will your response to them be.

It is, perhaps, the anticipation of those differences that make impending birth exciting. You get to improve your response to pregnancy, labor and delivery. You get to anticipate watching a new and different face and personality emerge. With each birth, you have the satisfaction of having lived and learned, and you hope your parenting skills will reflect your experience.

Yet just as there are differences, babies also share commonalities, similarities that I think I used to take for granted.

Until I did this again, I could only vaguely remember some of the things about babies I had promised myself I'd never forget.

Like the smell of a baby's head. And how perfectly that perfectly shaped head fits in the palm of my hand.

How a baby's tiny hand instinctively curls around your big finger. And how delicate are the nails on that hand.

How quickly your heart melts when your baby smiles at your face in recognition and unconditional love, especially and even after you've let her cry too long. And how unconditionally you love, too.

It was the expectation of differences that I talked about when I was pregnant.

Now that my new baby is here, I realize the similarities are what propelled me to do this again.

It is the differences in personality, eye color and sex that make my children unique.

But it is the universal similarities I love the most.

They are babies. And they're mine.

Clothes come in many sizes—except one that fits

Oct. 22, 1992

As if leaving a baby weren't traumatic enough, going back to work means I have to get dressed.

It's not that I've been wearing a nightgown and eating bon-bons since my second baby was born.

But neither have I had to face that closet.

An enclosure that looms the length of my bedroom, my closet is jam-packed with clothes in every stage of maternal life: maternity clothes, pre-maternity clothes, maternity clothes, post-maternity clothes and post-post-maternity clothes.

A daily encounter with that closet is a daily encounter with postpartum depression. Because stuffed as it is, nothing fits. Except, of course, the maternity clothes, which I refuse to wear. I would not survive someone asking, "When are you due?"

My rational self tells me this, too, shall pass. I just had a baby. I got my body back after the first baby. I'll get it back this time. I do want to wear a tucked-in blouse again someday. I do want to wear bras without double letters after the numbers. I do. I do. I do.

My obsessive-compulsive self compares my body at four months post-partum to women who snap back in two weeks. I see these bionic women, and I panic:

Not only will I never lose this weight, but I will lose control. I will gain even more.

In fact, if I try, I can dishearten myself at every turn.

I tell myself I'll just go shopping for another size of clothes.

But I can't stand the thought of looking in one of those three-sided mirrors.

I tried to psych myself up the other day by standing in front of a mirror at home and putting my hands on the parts of my body I don't like.

I didn't have enough hands.

I tried tilting up the mirror up to see how I'll look when I'm thinner.

All I could see was all the stuff hiding under the sagging parts.

I wish this didn't matter. I wish we celebrated our maternal bodies, showing off the Jell-O like the baby trophy it is.

I wish instead of panicking about weight, I'd spend more time thinking about what I have to show for it.

Their names are Emily and Christopher. She wears size 3 to 6 months. He wears size 4 years.

That would be the healthy attitude.

"We need to think, 'My body has done something truly fantastic. This is no small piece of work,'" said nurse-educator Rosemary Diulio, who works at the Maternity Center Association in New York.

"We need to focus on the fact that this is a gradual weight loss that occurs over a six-month period of time—MINIMUM. It can take a year. And it's not just weight loss; you have to get muscle tone back, too. Even then, I don't think your waist ever goes back to what it was. Basically what we have to do is learn to accept our new and changed bodies."

New and changed bodies.

Clothes manufacturers must love this. I imagine one day they'll even come out with a postpartum line.

But I won't have any more room in my closet.

Family is where you find it

Nov. 19, 1992

I could hardly contain my excitement when I heard that a 5-year-old girl was moving in next door with her mother.

After two years of living in a childless neighborhood, my son was finally going to have a playmate right next door.

But there was another, more selfish reason for my glee:

Tradeoffs.

My new neighbor could sit with my children while my husband and I ran out to dinner. I could sit with hers next time. She could send her child over to watch *Bambi* when she needed a break. I could send mine for an hour another night.

I tried to let my neighbor get moved in before I broached the topic. But she barely introduced herself when I said something, and I could tell by the flash in her eyes that she would have if I hadn't.

It's not that my neighbor and I don't like our kids. But we do like respite, the kind that extended family members provided a generation ago. In their absence, she and I have discovered that mutual relationships between friends and neighbors are one way to survive the stressed-out world of work, parenting and homemaking.

I didn't know about such relationships at first. Four years ago, when I became a parent for the first time, neither I nor anyone in my circle of young friends knew much about asking for help from anybody other than blood kin. I could only make long-distance phone calls to my mother and sisters, who could only listen from four states away.

But as adult life becomes more complicated, so does your approach to it. You learn to take help where you can find it and soon, giving and taking among neighbors, colleagues and friends becomes a way of life.

Whereas I operated in a vacuum after my first child was born, by the time I was postpartum with a second infant, I was a ready and willing participant in the "supper brigade" that I had helped form at work. For the first three weeks after I had my second baby, friends brought dinner in for my family, as we had begun to do for other families in our circle with new babies. Other friends appeared at my door with offers to wash my clothes, scrub my bathrooms and whisk away the older child so I could get used to the newer one.

My friends and I have slowly learned other ways to help each other. We make chicken soup for sick mothers and take kids to school when cars won't start. We have dinners together when our husbands are out of town on business. We've even formed a baby-sitting cooperative, trading colored pennies for each hour of baby sitting we provide each other.

I miss my children's grandmother, the one who in times past would have performed these services without asking or complaining. I bemoan the absence of aunts and uncles who are available to baby sit or at least ride my kids piggyback.

But I have developed a network of friends, who help fill in a lot of the holes the long lost, extended family can't anymore.

Together, we're redefining family. And we're finding it to mean many different things.

There's a little book that appears on the specialty shelf at the book store from time to time, usually around Valentine's Day.

It's called *A Family is a Circle of People Who Love You*.

It most certainly is.

Sick of doctor bills? Consider Dr. Mom

Dec. 3, 1992

I have threatened more than once to become a pediatrician.

Not that I could give much better care to my children, who are prone to chronic ear infections, allergies and other assorted childhood diseases.

But at least there would always be a doctor in the house.

No longer would I have to nag 4-year-old Christopher, "Is that an ear infection, or are you just scratching your ear like that to taunt me?" I could simply pull out my handy-dandy otoscope and see for myself. No more would I drag him on weekend emergency runs to the doctor's office for 25 percent more than the cost of a weekday visit. I'd be right there to diagnose and prescribe. Free. I wouldn't sit in a steamy bathroom at 4 in the morning anymore either, worrying that my child's croupy cough is something worse than a croupy cough.

I would know.

If I were a pediatrician, I would know everything. Finally, I would know the difference between a virus and bacteria, between a harmless rash and chicken pox, between expectorant and antihistamine.

Of course, there is a downside. There would be no more stickers from the receptionist.

I'd have to go to medical school.

And I'd be the one getting calls at midnight from people like me who start off by saying, "My child has been acting like this since 9 a.m., but for some reason I waited until midnight to call you."

Indeed, it must be at least as hard to be a pediatrician as it is to be a first-grade teacher.

Both not only have kids to deal with, they have kids' parents.

We're at the elbow at every visit, ready to tell doctors what we know, what we think we know and what we think they should know. And there are many such opportunities to tell them.

Checkups will total six before the child's first birthday, that is for kids whose parents follow guidelines set by the American Academy of

Pediatrics. Well-child visits are recommended again at 12 months, 15 months, 18 months and 24 months, then at 3 years, 4 years, 5, 6, 8, 10, 12, 14, 16, 18 and 20.

Unless the child is a descendant of Superman, there also will be sick visits to the doctor. Colds alone average six to 10. That's per year per child. There's likely to be a bronchitis here, a throw-up virus or two there, a strep throat, a broken arm or nose, chicken pox and ear infections—those damnable, tenacious ear infections, which attack 70 percent of all children at least once before they're 1. (Where did these things come from anyway?) A significant number of children will have such chronic problems with ears that there will be multiple visits to the doctor, the administering of expensive antibiotics and ultimately the insertion of little tubes into the ear canal while under anesthesia. Sometimes none of it works. In fact, you should consider yourself lucky if your child's ears respond to any of the above.

It's enough to make you want to become a pediatrician. Or study up on children's health and make recommendations to your doctor.

I understand there is a light at the end of the tunnel. Childhood germ-sharing and thus childhood illnesses lessen with age.

"Older kids generally aren't playing with each other in such a close fashion that they're smearing their hands on each other," says Dr. Steven P. Shelov, editor of *Caring for your Baby and Young Child: Birth to Age 5* and professor and vice chairman of pediatrics at the Albert Einstein College of Medicine and Montefiore Medical Center in the Bronx.

By that time, I'll be an expert.

At least I'll think so.

And my pediatrician will be more than ready for me to move on to another profession.

Dad steps in

Dec. 17, 1992

People around us smiled as my husband rushed to the table where I waited to have lunch with him the other day.

I was dressed in work clothes, obviously on lunch break from the office.

He was dressed in a rumpled pair of shorts and a half-tucked shirt. He had a 6-month-old clinging to his chest, a 4-year-old to his hand.

It was perhaps just as obvious that he had come from home. And I couldn't help but be proud.

They call him Mr. Mom.

House husband.

My partner.

Our lifeline.

Because my husband is a graduate student and a part-time college instructor, he can't be home with our children 9 to 5, five days a week. Our young son and daughter spend a few mornings a week at a child-care facility and a few hours during the week with me. But if you counted up all the hours in a work week, you'd find them spending most of their time with Daddy.

In our house, it's Daddy who spends long stretches of time wiping up juice and playing cars with one hand while changing diapers and shaking a rattle with the other. He's the parent who wonders if he's the only one in the house constantly picking up stuff from off the floor and putting it where it belongs. He's the one who gets frustrated when he can't finish a project, make a phone call, sit down for a minute because a 4-year-old is whining at his elbow.

I was afraid for us to try this at first. My husband isn't like me. He doesn't coo like a bird when our baby cries. He doesn't automatically scoop up our 4-year-old when he falls down. Nor does he happily hop up every time my son asks for juice, milk, a peanut butter and jelly sandwich or somebody to play with.

In fact, I was afraid my husband wouldn't hold up at all, that the situation would only add to the stress in our lives because he couldn't figure out exactly how to make his work fit around the kids or exactly what to do with the kids when he did.

I also knew there wouldn't be a whole lot of people out there with whom he could commiserate. Although the numbers have been increasing, stay-home fathers are still an aberration, which means isolation such as stay-home mothers have never seen.

Chris Stafford of New Brighton, Minn., knows. Stafford quit his job to stay home after the birth of his daughter, now 11. He also started a newsletter, called *Full-Time Dad*, which has introduced him to a lot of men like himself.

"The isolation definitely is the biggest problem, just not knowing anybody else doing what you're doing, not having anybody else to talk to," said Stafford, who also has a 7-year-old son. "I've talked to some fathers who dread stepping out the door. One person in Ohio says he walks outside and somebody says, 'Get a job.' He was helping his daughter's Brownie troop, and he got a call from the den mother's husband. He said 'We don't want you around here. You can't do this anymore. You're a strange guy.'"

Knowing what we might be up against, my husband and I nonetheless decided when I was pregnant with our second child that a child-care bill of $570 a month for two was too much. We didn't want a baby in a child-care center all day anyway. And my husband's job was flexible enough that we felt we had to exploit the opportunity.

It has not been a cakewalk. I've had to get used to the fact that just because he's not a woman doesn't mean he's incapable of caring for children. He's had to get used to me coming home every evening and grilling him.

But there are decided benefits.

Our kids get to be with one of their parents most of the time.

My husband gets to spend more time with our kids than a lot of fathers.

And there's nothing better than coming home to a husband who finally acknowledges:

"I don't know how mothers do it."

Just say no to holiday travel

Dec. 31, 1992

This time of year, families go on long trips to visit loved ones. Some families, that is.

When people asked where we were going for the holidays, my husband and I didn't flinch. Despite assorted relatives in five states, we knew what had to be done.

"We're not moving," we said.

Last year, traveling worked. We had one child who was at a magic traveling age—old enough that we didn't have to change diapers on our 750-mile trek to Grandma's and young enough that he didn't know he was in confinement.

This year, the 3-year-old has turned 4, which somehow makes him a) too old to sit in a car seat; b) too smart to be distracted by the same taped version of Winnie the Pooh played over and over; and c) just the right age to ask at every mile marker, "Where are we going?"

There's also this other traveler with us now. Reputed to be at an age when a ride around the block will put her to sleep, this particular baby is put in a car seat and immediately begins to arch her back in protest. And to scream.

Alas, this will not pass. It only gets worse, I hear, when the two kids begin talking to each other.

Traveling with more than one child is such an issue for today's on-the-go family that parenting gurus and pediatricians have devised elaborate schemes to counter the madness.

Parenting author John Rosemond suggests distributing "tickets" to kids before each trip. Every time the kids kick each other, scream at each other or say "Mommy, so-and-so won't stop pulling my hair, calling me names, sticking jelly beans down my pants," etc., a ticket is taken. If the family gets to the destination and the kids still have tickets left, they get to do something wonderful like go to the beach or to their favorite restaurant. If they don't have tickets left, they get to go to the hotel room and eat canned spinach or something equally unrewarding.

I've heard of other schemes—from administering sedatives (that one actually per the advice of a pediatrician), to stopping at shopping malls every couple of hours and letting the kids run off that boundless energy.

Last year's pre-Christmas trip, magically unchaotic as it turned out to be, was only thus because we broke it up into 2½ days when it could have been one. We also had the car organized like a filing cabinet.

Multiple types of food and traveling toys borrowed from a seasoned mother/traveler were arranged by category in the back seat. There was room for me to sit back there, so that when the youngest traveler began to squirm, I climbed beside him and began an entertainment and feeding frenzy— whatever worked.

A previously anxious mother of twin 1-year-old boys likewise was delighted that a little pre-planning—including lots of new Christmas toys for the return trip—rendered a 40-hour round trip to her mom's and dad's house a success.

But you never know.

There was the couple whose baby wouldn't be happy, no matter what Mom and Dad did. Eight hundred miles they drove to the tune of the baby's wails.

There was the 2½-year-old who screamed in protest when her mother left the backseat to take over the wheel from her exhausted father. Somewhere between New Jersey and Florida, she threw up blueberry yogurt all over the car.

I'm probably wimping out. But I'm not taking any chances.

Sorry, Grandma, but you know where to find us.

Mistakes are tough teachers

Jan. 14, 1993

My 4-year-old turned soulful eyes to me the other day and said, "You're a good mom, Mommy."

I didn't pay him to say that.

Nor did I buy off the stranger in the grocery store parking lot who must have heard me explain to Christopher why he shouldn't dart around cars.

"Most parents would have swatted his behind and never said a word," she stopped me to say.

Affirmation doesn't always come so cheaply. What's usually more immediately clear is when my parenting skills take a wrong turn.

Take what happened the other day.

Trying to finish up a long-distance call at home, I whispered to the preschooler at my elbow that he'd have to go away until I finished. He did all right.

In the time it took me to drop the phone, he had gone outside, gotten in my car and put it in reverse. Thank goodness a dip in the driveway forced the car to stop.

"But Mommy," he said, after we'd both caught our breath, "you told me to go away."

I have often wished for a definitive manual on raising children, a rule book that would tell me what to say and not to say, what to do and not to do, in my attempts to raise a man and not a monster.

I have wished for a parenting coach to call on, or a gauge, much like a thermometer, that I could stick under my child's arm to tell me how I'm doing as a parent.

Alas, there are no such tools. It's catch as catch can, and I'm the one with the mitt.

Affirmation helps, as does a child's behavior.

Nothing can raise my confidence more than having the only quiet child in the church pew. Likewise, it was a rewarding day for Mom and Dad when Christopher finally quit blurting, "Who's this?" when he answered the phone and started saying, "Who's calling, please?"

Aberrant behavior can tell you something needs to change, too.

"If your kid is running his head into the wall, then you need to do some boundary setting; something isn't going quite right," says Chicago-based parenting columnist Paul Rand. "If you're seeing dramatic behavior changes— if he was exuberant and outgoing and now he's morose and depressed, or if he gets clingy and he used to like being by himself—something is going on."

I learn by staring. Wherever I am, I scope out parents with their kids. If I like the way they look, I pay close attention to the way they act.

Unfortunately, I also learn by trial and error. And error—which makes parenting like anything else in life: It's the mistakes that teach the most immediate and lasting lessons.

For two days after Christopher tried to drive my car away, I walked around muttering, "I shouldn't have told him to go away. I shouldn't have told him to go away."

I doubt I ever will again.

Likewise, you learn very quickly that it's not good to yell only after you already hurt their feelings by yelling.

You learn to control your language only after they repeat "damn" after you.

You learn to be a good parent by being a bad one.

Of course, they can learn from your mistakes, too.

Because then they hear you say, "I'm sorry."

What do kids eat? Whatever's not on Mom's list

Feb. 4, 1993

In the beginning I was determined my child would eat only pure and healthy foods off the beaten path to McDonald's.

I fed him plain yogurt instead of ice cream, brown rice and lentils instead of meat.

Instead of Gerber's, my baby got pureed vegetables, many of them fresh from a friend's garden and flavored only with fresh garlic, and an assortment of fresh fruits, including kiwi and cantaloupe.

Even his first birthday cake was squeaky wholesome. Instead of giving in to a simple Duncan Hines with chocolate frosting into which he could happily plop his face, I spent hours hovering over a complicated cake that was sweetened with unsweetened apple juice and made especially dense with whole wheat flour and wheat germ.

No, none of that prefab stuff for us.

Then came Kraft macaroni and cheese.

And there's been no turning back.

From there, we have easily slipped into Tuna Helper and Chef Boyardee, Froot Loops and Kellogg's Frosted Flakes, fish sticks and red-dyed wieners straight out of the package.

My motto has switched from "All things pure and healthy" to "If it's easy and he'll eat it, clap your hands."

I don't know exactly when it was that I gave in.

It might have been the day I retrieved my toddler from a friend's house and found out that she unwittingly gave my normal American, naturally desirous child a piece of candy.

It might have been the 10th time he shouted/sang hysterically "Old MacDonald Had a Farm" and begged me to stop as we passed the golden arches. (I just know there was a conspiracy in the naming of that place.)

It might have been shortly after he learned to say "Ewyukky" when I put Jane Brody's latest concoction in front of him.

I suspect it was a gradual succumbing, to a world where expediency is key and where all the other kids have chocolate on their hands instead of carob.

(I must admit there's something to be said about the ease of pouring noodles into a pan of boiling water, then pouring cheese sauce over them 9 to 11 minutes later. And then he likes them. Every time. Guaranteed.)

This is not to say Christopher doesn't eat broccoli, squash or wheat berry bread anymore. But I have given up on being such a purist, on being the only mother who sends unfrosted, unsugared—and ultimately uneaten—muffins to my child's class when it's his birthday.

I still hold out hope that he will one day revert to trying anything and everything like he did when he was a baby. As the descendant of Deep Southerners on one side of the family and Middle Easterners who eventually settled into Cajun country on the other, I long for the day when he will eat beets, tabbouleh and seafood gumbo.

But for now, I'm resigned. If macaroni and cheese is all he'll eat, along with an occasional green bean, a "tree" of broccoli and/or a peanut butter and jelly sandwich—but only if it's cut in the shape of a sailboat—at least he's eating.

And if not, there's always Flintstone vitamins.

Gadgets—You gotta have 'em

Feb. 18, 1993

It's time to give credit where credit is due.

That being said, I would like to personally thank whoever invented the PLAYPEN, without which I might never go to the bathroom alone.

Besides making itself useful during pitstops and sudden phone calls, the playpen is essential in the mornings while I make the coffee, get the oatmeal and otherwise run in and out of view of 7-month-old Emily. Only in the playpen will I know she's safe from eating the stuff she always manages to find on the floor.

With all due respect to the consumer groups that tried to ban baby chairs on wheels, I would also like to express gratitude to the Consumer Products Safety Commission for keeping BABY WALKERS on the market so I could buy one, without which I could not make breakfast or dinner.

Although some babies get into trouble with their walkers, that is they "walk" them over to stairs and then fall down, my baby capably strolls around our stairless kitchen (but away from the stove, and there are no stairs) while I cook.

After the playpen and the walker, the next piece of equipment that engages my baby during any given day at home is the much-appreciated CRIB, where she likes to lie and stare up at her hypnotize-me-to-sleep MOBILE.

The crib, considered standard in the homes of most babies, is nonetheless critical, not just for sleeping but because it keeps Emily safely and happily caged for a few minutes before and after each snooze.

After nap time, while I am having clean-the-kitchen time, Emily goes into the true godsend, the BACKPACK, after which there might be the family outing. And because Mom's back is now hurting, Dad takes over baby, whom he puts in a SLING because he doesn't like the backpack—perhaps because she likes to pull hair while she's in it.

After the outing, there often is the bath, which means TEDDY TUBS, a thick piece of sponge that sits immobile on the bottom of the otherwise dangerous bathtub. Here, Emily will be content to sit until the cows come home or until her little feet get more wrinkled than they already are.

This is not to mention numerous occasions in the safety-first CAR SEAT. Nor does this assessment of the baby gadgetry in our home include a full explanation of the MECHANICAL SWING, not to be confused with the DOORWAY SWING, which is of prime importance when Emily is tired but has convinced herself she's not.

During any given day, Emily will also spend time in the back-saving CHANGING TABLE, the belted HIGH CHAIR and the INFANT CARRIER so that by the time Emily goes night-night, she has been entertained, cuddled and harnessed by more than a dozen gadgets and pieces of equipment.

Such modern-day accouterments might seem overindulgent, if not overcrowding, to some, especially people who don't have a baby, who invite people who do have a baby to their house and then watch as they bring in armloads of stuff.

But those of us modern-day moms who have a baby or who have ever had one—we know. Without the various gadgets and baby equipment that occupy big spaces in every room of the house, we might have to—gasp—entertain, cuddle and/or harness the baby all by ourselves.

There are those who might say, "Hey, Grandma did it without a baby monitor."

But whatever gets you through the night.

And, hey, poor Grandma.

This time, I know how to change a diaper

March 4, 1993

One of the best things about having a second child is having prior knowledge.

The first go-round, you don't know how quickly you will change—from someone who used to sleep in to someone who forgets how, from someone who used to spend uninterrupted time on the phone to someone who can't get a word in edgewise, from someone who used to dine out to someone who doesn't dare.

You know going in the second time to expect these things. Because you are these things.

If you're lucky, your second child will reap the immediate benefit of other lessons you had to learn the hard way the first time. For example, I already knew the second time:

• How to change a diaper.

When I was in the hospital alone for the first time with my firstborn and unable to stop his crying, I buzzed for the nurse, who asked me if he was hungry, did he want his pacifier, did I check his diaper. Diaper? This time I knew, without a nurse having to demonstrate, that the tabs fasten in the front.

• To let my husband take care of the baby.

I know now that if I tell my husband he's not doing it right or if I act like I am the only one who knows how to take care of the baby, he'll begin to believe me.

• Not to panic every time the baby's head feels hot.

I still get embarrassed when I think about the time I called the doctor at midnight, only to learn that my firstborn was warm because I was holding him next to me.

• Not to worry so much about potty training.

• Not to worry so much about child care.

• Not to worry so much, period.

It's OK if you don't change the crib sheet every time the baby's nose runs on it. You just turn it upside down.

It's OK if a baby cries himself—but briefly, in my book—to sleep. In fact, I've learned the hard way that rocking and nursing a baby to sleep every single night will only result in having a baby who has to be rocked and nursed to sleep every single night.

It's OK to call my child's blanket a "bankie" and otherwise use baby talk. Just like my 4-year-old, the second baby eventually will grow up, too, using proper English, and without infantile tendencies, despite my sugary-sweet ones.

Most importantly, I know the baby probably will survive. I will not drop her.

They told my husband and me that having more than one child would be harder. And in some ways, it is.

Having more than one child means being pulled in more than one direction. When one's getting over an ear infection, the other one's just getting one. When one wants to nurse quietly in the dark, the other wants me to pretend I'm the Beast and he's Gaston.

Forget this stuff about the children entertaining each other. One day, maybe, they'll play for hours while my husband and I sip wine and discuss events of the day. As for now, they've yet to play more than 30 seconds together since one wants to play with the Fisher-Price people and the other wants to eat them.

Yet, despite being even more deprived of sleep, adult conversation and spontaneous nights on the town, I know something this time that I didn't know before.

I can do this.

The call of pinafores and lace

April 22, 1993

I try to avert my eyes and walk very quickly when I find myself nearing a certain section of the department store.

It's not the section where they sell the Russell Stover candies. Nor is it the lingerie department or the counter where clerks in heavy makeup try to convince you that you want to look like them.

It's the section where they sell the itsy, bitsy swimsuits with ruffles on the behind. It's the racks upon racks of delicate dresses bearing labels that say, "Radishes and Roses" and "Warm Hearts" that tempt me to the brink of an unbalanced checkbook.

I must point out here that I consider myself an enlightened woman who said she'd never, ever gender-type her daughter by placing too much attention on what she wears.

As a matter of fact, I had promised myself when I became a mother almost five years ago that I wouldn't obsess about what any of my kids, boys or girls, wore as long as they appeared clean and neat. For his first two years, I dressed my son in almost nothing but hand-me-downs from friends, family and secondhand stores. I saved his clothes for the anticipated next child, too, painstakingly packing them away into boxes in the top of my closet as Christopher outgrew them.

But enlightened or not, something happens when you have a little girl, especially if you've heretofore dressed only little boys. Boy clothes are boring: T-shirts and shorts for summer. Sweat pants and sweat shirts for winter. White socks. A jacket. The only cutesy things on the racks for boys are sailor suits at Easter, which they will begin denouncing by age 3.

After the experience of boys' clothes, gaining entry to the girls' department is like getting a key to the Magic Kingdom. Little girls' clothes are a fairyland full of sugar and spice and grace and beauty—and an impulsive person's nightmare. Do you want strawberries on the hem and smocking on the bodice or smocking on the hem and strawberries on the bodice? Do you want a dress or a romper? Seersucker or a poly-cotton blend? A one-piece or two?

With so many choices, the mother of a daughter is pressed to study the girls' department every time she sniffs one out. One department store clerk who's been selling girls' clothes for 17 years told me she frequently watches as mothers march right past the girls' department, then turn around and march right back.

"People have said they come in here to look for something for themselves and they end up in the girls' department," she told me.

The clerk couldn't begin to speculate why we do this to ourselves and our daughters, although I wonder if maybe we're reliving our girlhoods, when we dressed ourselves and our dolls in pinafores and lace. Perhaps just as accurately, we're shifting years of impulse buying from ourselves to our girls, who in turn will shift it to their girls and so on and so on.

I must say, despite the allure, I usually only browse longingly, partly because my friends also have little girls who pass along their outgrown "Radishes and Roses" to Emily.

That's usually. While the clerk and I talked last week, I hardly noticed as I slipped two marked-down sundresses onto the counter, one of them in irresistible mint-green pin stripes with ballet slippers on the front and the other in a sun-yellow seersucker appliqued with a floppy-eared bunny.

Ah well. Even if I'm unsuccessful at teaching Emily that clothes do not, in fact, make the woman, at least I'll teach her to get them off the sales rack.

The unstoppable march of time

May 6, 1993

I stare long and hard into the eyes of my children. I write down what they say and do. I take a lot of pictures, filing them meticulously into photo albums and taking them out often to look at.

But try as I might, I can't make them stay the way they are.

Right now, I'm the mother of little children.

The elder is 4, dubbed by one expert a "golden year" for children and a rewarding year for parents.

Capable, yet desperate for our approval, he strives always to be a good boy who can do everything we've taught him all by himself.

He is sociable, curious, an open book determined to fill his pages and in love with everything, including his mom and dad. Still.

The other night he shifted all the toothbrushes around in the holder and when I asked him why, he told me it was because he wanted his to be next to mine.

As for the 10-month-old, she thinks she's part of me.

She moves away from me to explore her environs, but checks back often to see that I'm watching. She cackles when her eyes meet mine.

When I carry her about the house, which I can easily do because she weighs a mere 18 pounds, she keeps one delicate hand lightly placed on my chest.

She knows few words. Rather, she expresses herself with her body and her smiles, many of which she gives to me.

Together, they are a dance of siblings, who seem at this point to only love each other. She follows him with her eyes and howls pitifully when she realizes she can't find him. In the mornings, they like to roll around on the bed together and laugh.

But it's not just their purity that makes this time special.

It's mine.

It's the way I feel, innocent and unknowing, unknowledgeable.

I don't know yet whether we'll have to borrow for college. I don't know yet whether I've made any big mistakes raising them.

Neither of them is anything right now but a child, which leaves me space and time to dream of what will be instead of fretful that they aren't just like I had hoped.

All good parents encourage their children to grow up and out. At times we long for that maturity. For along with young children comes frustration, especially in the early years of a child's life, when the nights are long and the days are, too.

We wish she would sleep through the night, get over the ear infections and get down and walk instead of squirm in our arms.

We wish that he could turn on his own cartoons on Saturday mornings, make his own peanut-butter-and-jelly sandwiches.

But along with growing maturity comes the real stuff of parenting.

We are perched now on the precipice of decisions, between public kindergarten and private, between lunch money and homemade sandwiches, between Cub Scouts and music lessons. We are a step away from dealing with sibling rivalry and bad influences we can't control.

All of which makes me think of a story a mother told me about her son who was 4 at the time and late getting up and out of the house one day.

He realized he wasn't going to make it to a much-anticipated appointment. But then with his wide-open mind and his innocent heart, he remembered his mom had changed the clock a while back for daylight saving time.

And he came up with what he thought was the perfect solution.

"Mommy, you can stop the clock!" he told her.

If only we could.

"Vacation with kids" is an oxymoron

June 3, 1993

After a year and a half of boycotting interstate travel, my husband and I finally went on vacation as a family of four, to visit my mother and three sisters in New Orleans.

Having done so, having spent two weeks at the home of one of those sisters, a childless woman who still doesn't know what hit her, we came to this conclusion: Not only do you not travel with young children. You never go on vacation.

You might go on a trip. But not a "vacation" in the purest sense of the word, which has its roots in the Latin *vacare*, to be at leisure.

Merely packing up the kids for an extended visit to another person's home is hard work, as you attempt to manipulate the contents of their toy box and chest-of-drawers into a few suitcases.

While some might see this as obsessive overpacking, you are actually acting quite smartly to stave off daily laundry and the irksome "Mommy, I'm bored" hundreds of miles from home.

But don't think just because you had the foresight to pack the portable crib, the baby backpack, the attention-keeping balls and coloring books, toy cars and rattles, the baby food and teething rings, you get to collapse on the bed once you reach your destination.

Living safely and sanely with kids in a place other than home requires constant vigilance, particularly if the place is not accustomed to children.

I spent a great deal of time snatching the baby away from exposed electrical outlets, cat food bowls and unfamiliar porch edges. More than once, I was forced to apologize to my shell-shocked sister, for the treasured figurine on the floor, the baby crying in the night, the glops of baby food left on the kitchen table.

Likewise, new rules for new environs had to be established—and worse, enforced—for our 4-year-old son.

No, I had to keep reminding him, you can't play on the sidewalk by yourself in the middle of a big city. No, you can't have ice cream every time one of your doting aunts wants to take you out. And quit using your uncle's souvenir flag from Switzerland as a baseball bat.

When you're on vacation with kids, you put away your own hopes and dreams. You forgo memories of vacations past, of the relaxing honeymoon by train into Canada in the late summer six long years ago.

Remember, honey?

Remember long bicycle rides through the streets of Montreal? Remember romantic, late-night meals, just you and me? Remember uninterrupted hours speaking French with the Quebec locals and quiet nights reading side by side?

When you're a parent on vacation, you seek out restaurants that serve green beans and macaroni and cheese. Or you stay in and eat Ragu, just like home.

We managed to cajole a few hours of baby sitting out of my family during our trip. But visions of family members demanding, "Here, we'll take the kids. Go! Go!" every night never materialized.

Sleeping in? Are you kidding? Our baby's sleep habits were worse than ever, what with that thin mattress that comes with the porta-crib.

Leisure reading? I kept eyeing my novel sitting on the bedside table. I picked it up once for five minutes, in between retrieving the baby after her nap and cleaning up the latest mess in my sister's living room before her husband came home.

Vacationing with kids gives new meaning to "home away from home."

There's no escape.

In Barney's defense

July 1, 1993

I am coming out of the closet with an unpopular opinion I would never utter aloud on a crowded bus:

I like Barney.

Wait. As long as I'm emerging:

I love Barney.

I have been enamored of the happy *Tyrannosaurus rex* ever since last summer when my son and I accidentally discovered his simple messages and harmless nature during the half-hour slot after "Sesame Street."

Such a positive emotional response makes me a sap among peers, to wit: Mention Barney in a group of parents with Barney-mad preschoolers, and everyone will hold their nose, say "Pew-wee!" or mimic the "I love you, you love me" song.

My friends are riding a nationwide bandwagon of Barney-bashing that has David Letterman doing the Top 10 Horrifying Secrets of Barney the Dinosaur, *The New York Times* describing him as a "talking eggplant" and *The Washington Post* saying he looks like a "newt with dentures." There's more: A radio talk show staged a mock Barney execution. And a Florida man, the father of a 2½-year-old Barney lover, started the "I Hate Barney Secret Society," a two-page newsletter that takes shots at the show with its "damned theme song."

As a parent who was immediately taken with Barney and the multi-ethnic boys and girls who follow him around for half an hour, singing, playing, learning and creating, I'm perplexed.

"Barney & Friends," watched by two million children every weekday on more than 200 TV stations, delivers educational themes and simple messages about friendship, family, health and safety that children can understand and readily apply to life.

With all due respect to another award-winning show, "Sesame Street," which uses double entendres, adult humor and Bruce Springsteen sound-alikes to relate to preschoolers, Barney and his friends sing songs my child can remember and sing. Barney uses repetition and the familiar to get points across.

One of the last episodes I saw was about bugs. Segments included Barney's pals dancing in butterfly wings to Tchaikovsky's "The Nutcracker Suite." The children made a spider web and a spider out of construction paper and glue. One of them told the story of the worker ant and the lazy grasshopper, which was followed by a song about ants. They sang "Itsy-Bitsy Spider" and recited the nursery rhyme, "Little Miss Muffet."

At the end of the show, as always, Barney spent 30 seconds highlighting the show. And he and the kids sang that "I love you" song together.

Parents say they don't like it.

So? They're not supposed to.

Simplicity, repetition, familiarity and singing along—those are things kids like, relate to and learn from.

The wife of the Florida father who launched the newsletter says she tries to divert her child's attention to "something more broadening, you know, like 'Sesame Street.' "

Do the kids need broadening? Or do we?

My friends say Barney and his pals are too sweet and wholesome. Since when are sweet and wholesome not admirable attributes for children? What do we want? "Beavis & Butthead?"

That Barneyism is a cult, as one father suggested to *The Wall Street Journal*, is as silly to me as Barney is to him. How long does he think the attention span of a preschooler is, anyway? If that father is being a good parent, he is exposing his child to other cultural experiences so that he doesn't become one-dimensional.

I love Barney because I've seen how excited my child gets when he remembers the words to the songs Barney and the kids sing—yes, over and over and over. For a long time, there were only 30 episodes. That number has expanded, although for whom, I don't know. I doubt the kids noticed.

Come on. Let's lighten up and give the poor guy a break. Not to mention the millions of little kids who mean it when they sing "I love you" back to the goofy purple dinosaur.

I'm going home

July 15, 1993

After five years of holding subscription rights to *Working Mother* magazine, my status and that of the rest of my family is about to change.

In the same month this spring, almost in the same week, my husband finished graduate school and accepted a job. Poof.

Now I'm quitting mine. I'll still write. But I'll write at home on the weekends, during the kids' naps and at night when they're in bed.

No more will I iron work clothes with a baby on my ankles and then hustle her and her brother to child care so that I can skulk into work, sheepish, because everybody else always seems to get there before I do.

No more will I worry that my boss is going to need me as I'm hurrying out the door to take a sick child to the doctor.

No more will I cry when a favorite caregiver quits.

I will be the favorite caregiver.

I will go to the park and join a play group. I will bake muffins, lots and lots of them, blueberry and banana, apple cinnamon and honey nut. I will hug my kids at 10 in the morning and 4 in the afternoon and sit in the dirt and write their names with a stick. I will take naps with the kids. In the middle of the day. Every day.

This is not a dream. Well, maybe a bit of one; my stay-home mother friends are quick to tell me that staying home with kids isn't the nirvana I fantasize.

But being a full-time working mother doesn't come close, not for me, not now. It's going to one all-consuming job in the morning and another at night—sometimes all night when a child is sick. It's feeling pulled in too many directions. It's too much, for me.

Some mothers don't mind the added stress of working full time. They like working outside the home, and they have good support systems, to include stable child care, understanding supervisors and involved husbands. Many working women I know say they wouldn't enjoy staying home all day with their kids; they say they would be doing their kids a disservice by pretending.

Other working mothers feel trapped. They're afraid to leave the work force for any length of time for fear that potential employers will point up their absence when they try to return. Some women feel they have to keep working because they're all too aware of the possibility of divorce, which could leave them high and dry if they don't have a job to fall back on. Some mothers work because they have to eat and pay rent.

I'm very, very lucky. My husband and I promised ourselves a long time ago that we wouldn't let money concerns overtake concerns about our emotional health and well-being. Knowing full well that our family would be better off financially with both of us working, we nonetheless agreed that I would consider slowing down my professional pace after he finished graduate school and got a job.

During his years in school, I fantasized about what slowing down might mean. Maybe I'd give up my outside work interests all together and focus completely on home and hearth.

But when it came time, I realized that not only did I not want to give up the career I'd spent more than a decade building, I didn't have to. Even as I struggled these past few years as a working mother, I also gained professional maturity and independence, enough that I think I can quit my job to focus more on my family and still maintain my writing career on my own.

I hope I'm not deluding myself.

I hope, too, that I never again lose control over the balance knob in my life.

I hope one more thing, as I prepare to move closer to the other side.

I hope I never, ever judge full-time working mothers as I have been judged these past few years by people who think all mothers can and should quit their jobs and go home.

Whether a mother—or a father—stays home or works outside the home is way too complicated and personal for anybody else to pass judgment.

The bottom line is commitment, as my kids' pediatrician, a mother of two, suggested earlier this week when I rushed the baby in for one of those pre-work doctor's appointments. People who work outside the home can be just as committed to their children as people who don't. Trust us.

For right now, quitting my full-time job is the answer. For me. For my family. For right now, I'm going home. And I can't wait.

Good-bye tinged with hope and sadness

July 29, 1993

We said good-bye a few weekends ago to the upstate South Carolina town where I grew up.

We went to Christopher's great-grandmother's house, where I lived the first six months after I was born, where my 80-year-old grandmother now lies in her living room in a hospital bed, bedridden from a stroke.

We went to the grave of my father, who died two years ago, when Christopher was 2½, before my second child, his first blood granddaughter, was conceived.

We even went to see the backyard of the house where I lived from the time I was six months old until I was 15. The famous backyard. It really was big. The people who live there now let me walk back and show Christopher the place where my father built the tree house for his four daughters and the way-back place in the yard that is still rolling from where he plowed it for a garden. I showed Christopher where my sisters and I used to play baseball, eat watermelon, swing.

Bittersweet is a word I've always liked. It's a word I thought of a lot that weekend as I said good-bye to things that aren't really there anymore. It's a word I've thought of more and more during the last couple of months, ever since my husband finished graduate school and accepted a job.

His accepting the position means he finally gets to do what he wants, that is, work hard outside the home at a job that is challenging and stimulating. I get to do what I want now, too, that is, take a break for a while professionally, take control of our family and our home.

His accepting the position also means we have to say good-bye, because his new job is in another state.

South Carolina is where I grew up. It's the place I left with my mother and sisters 20 years ago and a decade later, came back to. It's where I matured professionally, working almost all these 10 years at the same place. South Carolina is where I met and married my husband. It's where we had our children, one of them in the bedroom of the house where we live now.

This is where we have our mechanic, our haircutter, our pediatrician, our preschool. It's where we have our baby sitter, our children's godparents, our neighborhood, our friends. This is where my children have roots, deep ones that go back to great-great grandparents on both sides of my family.

We are trying to figure out how to say good-bye.

My husband and I hurry to last-minute gatherings with various collections of friends and trade off the kids so we can go to lunch with colleagues.

For Christopher we have planned a going-away, hot-dog party with some of his preschool classmates. To help him understand the timing of the move, we've put up a calendar at home, at just the right height for a 4-year-old. Several times a day, he counts down the days to Aug. 7, which is marked, "Go to Florida." He always stops at Aug. 7, because that's as far as the calendar goes.

We look forward to what's beyond. And still, it's bittersweet, made more so by a child, who's been waking up in the middle of the night. And when I ask him what's wrong, he half-mumbles, half-moans: "I'm excited."

He moves back and forth, from sleep to so excited he can't sleep, from sad because he won't get to have his September birthday party at the local roller rink now, to manic because he's going to get his very own room in our new and bigger place.

His emotions and actions are raw, pure and raw, so that when we went to his great-grandmother's house, he refused to go in because she looked so bad. So pure and raw that when we visited my father's grave, he suddenly sat down with his back to me, on top of the plaque that identifies the place where his grandpa is buried.

"Ask me what I'm doing, Mom," he said," turning his head so one eye could see me.

"What are you doing, honey?"

"Sitting on Poppy's lap," he said.

Ah, children. We move on. We look for ways to say good-bye. They help us.

Strangers in a strange land

Aug. 25, 1993

What with playground equipment that's too high, bicycles that are too fast and strangers lurking on every corner with germs on their hands, there was already plenty for a parent to be phobic about.

Now come gators.

We have been uprooted and transplanted to a place where 2,000-pound creatures with mouths the size of small station wagons roam the land looking for little children.

This might be an exaggeration. But if it is, I don't know by how much.

The weekend in June that my husband and I came to Florida looking for a place to live, we read in the local paper about a tragic alligator attack.

We tried to believe it was a one-in-a-million incident like everybody said it was. But then after we had moved, several weeks later, there was another one-in-a-million incident.

Unfortunately our 4-year-old, with the vivid imagination familiar to his age group, heard about these incidents, so that he frequently reminds us that we've moved to a jungle.

His questions as we explore our new environs aren't so much, "Are we ever going to find any friends?" and, "Where's the closest Discovery Zone?" as much as, "Do you promise there aren't any gators over there?" as he crawls up his father's leg.

Even without his constant reminders, we can't help but be hyper-alerted ourselves to the fact that the University of Florida doesn't call its football team the Fighting Gators for nothing.

At the entryway to every speck of water around—and there's no scarcity in Florida—there are little wooden signs etched with tiny alligators and the warning, "No pets."

A nice young man guarding one of the lakes told me the no-pet clause is because little dogs tend to run up and down the shoreline, yapping, which tends to attract hungry gators. Wouldn't that go for babies, too, I asked, clutching mine closer to my chest.

It's true that there was plenty more than gators—which I hear run 30 miles an hour and sport 160 teeth—to obsess over as we moved a family of four across state lines.

We could have spent a great deal of time wondering when Christopher will ever settle down from all the changes in his young life and how we're going to get him into a good preschool in the middle of August.

We could have worried about the effects of changing roles on me and my husband. After six years, he's the one working full time outside the home and I'm the one who's trying her hand at working and taking care of the kids at the same time—inside the home.

An even better worry would be the one about health insurance, which we were without for a month as we waited for my husband's to kick in before the baby's ear infections did.

We also could have done some fact-finding to discover that alligators probably really only run 5 mph. And like bees, bears and other creatures of the wild, if you don't bother them, they won't bother you. This is nesting season for alligators. They nest in the weeds near shorelines. If you don't step into the weeds, they won't cross you.

But it was hard to focus on any of these things when we were busy teaching Christopher to run zigzag.

Gators don't know how to run straight. So if one starts running after you, you're supposed to run zigzag.

So now when we talk about Stranger Danger, I've got to add, "And run zigzag if you ever see a gator coming after you."

This isn't the home state of Disney World.

We are living in Jurassic Park.

I found the scissors!

Sept. 9, 1993

Something strange is happening to my kitchen floor.

It's clean. I clean it. Several times a day, I get down on my hands and knees, and I wipe up the spills and dirt left by two small children and their two large parents.

I know what's in all the Tupperware containers in the refrigerator, too. What's more, the leftovers inside them get eaten because I remember to get them out and offer them to people.

There's the laundry. It gets done. Several times in the last few weeks I have looked in the hamper and found nothing in it. Nothing rotting in the washer waiting for the dryer. Nothing in the dryer. Everything had been folded and put away.

Cleanliness and household organization had never been a strong suit in our house before, the easy excuse being that my husband and I had other things to do—working full-time jobs and/or going to school, taking care of two kids, sleeping. Our incomes didn't come close to affording a housekeeper. Translate: About the only time our house came close to clean was when we were expecting company. And with two young children, that wasn't very often.

Like many couples, my husband and I talked, often very loudly, about housework. Like many couples, we concocted elaborate plans.

One time we agreed we'd make do during the week, and after work on Fridays we'd deep clean.

We had a great time that one Friday night, cranking up the stereo and dancing around the house with the kids while we Spic 'n' Spanned.

But the following Friday, he had a business appointment during our appointed cleaning time. And the next, I had had a hard week at work and just couldn't get pumped up for three hours of scheduled cleaning.

An oft-quoted survey by the Good Housekeeping Institute placed housekeeping near the bottom of the priority list for most families today.

Housekeeping wasn't even making our list.

I had decided we were slobs.

Then, a few weeks ago, I quit my full-time job to work part time from home. And I happily slid into the abyss of domestic engineering.

Not only did I go about the daily duties of toilet bowls and laundry with great energy and aplomb, but I caught myself humming as I alphabetized the long-neglected spice rack and organized the overflowing bulletin board. Joyfully, I sorted through the coupons, finally throwing away the stuck-together ones marked, "Expires September 1987." Gladly, I rearranged overstuffed closets and drawers. With particular delight, I rediscovered the elusive light bulbs and AAA batteries and put them in their place.

They tell me the thrill of changing TP rolls has been known to wane. That past tendencies to pay greater attention to other things will renew themselves once the novelty of being home wears off.

Already one morning this week I passed a pile of Lucky Charms somebody left on the floor and I didn't even pick them up.

Which is too bad. After all these years of disarray, I had found solace in the intimate corners of our home where nobody else dared to go. I had found life in the nooks and crannies that heretofore had been choked with broken pencils and pretzel crumbs.

When somebody needed something, I knew where to find it. When people came over, their feet didn't stick to the kitchen floor.

For a time, I had rediscovered the lost art of housekeeping.

For a time, however brief, I actually knew where the scissors were.

Accidents happen

Sept. 23, 1993

At some point after you become a parent, you child-proof your house.

You lock up the Drano in the utility room and remember to turn pot handles to the back of the stove. You start disposing of old razors somewhere other than the indoor waste basket and plug up the electrical sockets with those little plastic things.

You're diligent, at first. But after a while, after nothing happens, you might loosen up some.

You might let a dry cleaner bag slip into the house.

You might move the Drano to a more convenient shelf in the kitchen.

You might forget to tighten the child-resistant cap on a bottle of medicine and then leave it within reach.

Emily had been sitting in the kitchen sink. At 14 months, she loves to sit in the kitchen sink, facing the cold water faucet and pouring water from one measuring cup to the other.

I was in the same room, doing laundry. I'd gather an armload of clothes from the washer, throw it into the dryer, look up to see that she was OK.

Gather an armload, throw it in, look up.

Gather, throw, look.

There was nothing for her to hurt herself on.

She couldn't turn on the hot water.

The only thing on the counter was a basket of medicines.

I was in the same room.

I was watching her.

But when I stopped what I was doing to get a closer look, I found Emily clutching a bottle of medicine. Its "child-resistant" cap was off. The bottle, which had held at least 30 antihistamine tablets, was empty. And there was a ring of white around my baby's mouth.

The Poison Control Center operator told me when I called that more than two of the pills that curbed my allergies so well could poison my young daughter. Get her to the emergency room now, he said.

In 1992, the year this incident occurred, poison control centers received one million calls involving children under 6 who'd ingested poison. Poison control phone operators were able to handle most of those calls over the phone; parents were told to administer syrup of Ipecac to induce vomiting, for example.

But 154,000 of those cases received medical attention. Either the child ingested something particularly dangerous or in a particularly large amount, or the parent didn't know how much or what the child had ingested.

Of the children who required medical treatment, 29 died, one of them a 3-year-old boy who drank mouthwash. One and one half ounces was all he drank.

As it turns out, Emily never showed any signs of toxicity, which indicated that most of the bitter-tasting pills, if not all of them, went down the drain. I can only guess that she clapped her hand over her mouth while she was playing with the dissolving tablets, which is why her mouth was ringed with white when I found her.

But because nobody knew how many pills Emily had taken and because an overdose of this particular drug had been known to cause seizures and heart irregularities, my daughter had to be treated as if she had been poisoned.

She had to be held down while an emergency room nurse forced her to drink activated charcoal. A gooey, black liquid that is as hideous as it sounds, it binds itself to the poison so the body will excrete it. Because of the potentially long-lasting effects of the antihistamines, Emily also had to be admitted to the pediatric intensive care unit for 24 hours for monitoring. She was poked and prodded, hooked up to a heart monitor and an IV needle in case she needed emergency drugs and made to stay overnight in a ward full of very ill children, some of whom were dying.

All because of my carelessness.

Despite the happy outcome, it was a terrible ordeal for Emily. And for her family. During those first several hours when we weren't sure what was going to happen, I felt fear and guilt so intense I couldn't even make a pact with God. I thought my baby was going to die.

Because of something I'd done.

I have quit feeling guilty. I have learned that accidents happen, even to the best of us, even to people who are trained to know better. My pediatrician thought his 20-month-old son ate dishwashing powder under his watch. Luckily, it turned out that the toddler was only playing with the overturned box. But the baby still had to be put to sleep so doctors could determine whether his esophagus was burned.

This is why the American Academy of Pediatrics suggests keeping corrosives like Drano way out of the reach of children. In a worst-case scenario, doctors would have had to remove that toddler's esophagus and put part of his colon in its place.

I have learned that lots of us think lots of the stuff we keep around the house is innocuous. Many people keep iron pills around the house for anemia. But as few as 10 pills will kill a child after slowly eating the lining of his stomach and intestinal tract. Iron pills are the leading cause of poisoning death in children, according to the National Capital Poison Center at Georgetown University Hospital in Washington.

Emily's story could have had a tragic outcome like so many others. I instead tell the story of a life lesson, of being prodded, so that when Emily and I returned home from the hospital, I scoured the house, eliminating all the hazards I'd eased up on. My husband had already put the basket of medicines out of reach.

What happened to Emily was terrible. But it reawakened my sense of responsibility to my children.

I'm here not just to teach them good manners, good eating habits and how to develop a healthy mental attitude. It's most essential that I keep their little worlds safe for them, especially when they can't.

Accidents happen. I'm glad I quit feeling guilty. I hope I never quit feeling responsible.

Vows to a second-born

Oct. 7, 1993

I vowed when I became pregnant for the second time that the new baby would get equal treatment, equal time and a personalized, needlepoint wall hanging.

Ha. Unlike her first-born brother, whose own wall hanging is on the wall across from his bed, the needlepoint kit of my second-born child is sitting in a plastic bag in the bottom of my closet with three rows of Xs stitched in it.

There is absolutely no excuse for this glaring inequity. But there is a reason: Birth order.

You can refute the hype all you want, which has stocked popular book shelves in recent years with such titles as *First Born, Second Born, Unlocking the Secrets of Your Birthright and Relationships* and *The Birth Order Book, Why You Are the Way You Are.* The authors of these books tell us that first-borns, with all that first-time parent attention heaped on them, often turn out to be perfectionists, over-achievers and 52 percent of U.S. presidents. Second-borns, left to their own devices by parents who are too busy making mistakes on the first-born, are independent and so determined to get along they forget about their own needs. Last-borns, surrounded by people who cater to them, struggle with self-centeredness and an aversion to responsibility.

You can set your mind against such generalities, refusing to believe that your child's personality will be made or broken on whether she was born in 1988 or 1992.

What you can't dismiss are sheer logistics and the fact that you didn't have any children when you had the first one, and now you do. There were no little hands to grab the needle out of your hand the first go-round, and now there are.

Of course, you love them just the same.

But during the first year of the second child's life, a great deal of energy is spent making sure the first child is OK with this new person in the house.

By the time you realize the second baby is a person, too, it's too late. The fate of her needlepoint hanging has already been established, as has her second-born, I-can-take-care-of-myself personality.

Whereas the first baby was hovered over with a first-aid kit, a washcloth and a camcorder, the second baby is carried around in a football hold while you chase the first. When you realize you're actually carrying a baby, you smile down at her and say some cooing word. She smiles back and you go back to chasing.

You sort of check in with the second.

Of course, being second-born has its advantages. Those mistakes do get made on someone else. Second-borns usually learn to hold a spoon, go potty and sing "Twinkle, Twinkle, Little Star" a lot faster than first-borns; they've got another little person to emulate. Second-borns are prone to being easy-going and adaptable, content in almost any situation, independent, because they've had to be.

I know about second-borns. My mother tells me I fared quite well as one, despite also being sandwiched, between my first-born sister that was born 11 months before me and a second sister who came four years later. By the time a third sister came along two years after that, I was well on my way to creating my own little world. To this day, my mother still tells people I don't have any problems. I was the "easy" one, she says.

I look at Emily, and I wonder if she's learning to be the easy one, too.

Maybe she won't even notice that Christopher got a rocking horse wall hanging stitched with his name, birth date and weight, and she didn't.

I also look at Emily, and I see me. I see a little girl who notices but doesn't say anything because she's the easy one.

I look at Emily and I think maybe one day, I'll dig out that needlepoint and I'll start stitching on it again, one X at a time.

Something positive about child care

Oct. 21, 1993

During five years as a full-time working mother, I learned a lot about child care.

I learned that it doesn't feel so good putting a young baby in child care. I learned that too few caregivers and too many children often signify bad child care, and that there's a lot of it out there. I learned to expect anything, that a child-care center can close for two weeks during Christmas and still demand payment.

Ultimately, I found something that surprised me. I found something positive about child care.

These positives have names.

In our family, the first of these was a woman we call Ammi Mary.

In the mornings, her classical music playing in the background, she introduced 4-month-old Christopher to books. In the afternoons, with Christopher sitting on her lap on our front porch, she introduced him to nature, pointing out the squirrels and the birds that lived in the trees. Without even knowing it, perhaps, Ammi Mary taught me, too. Watching this mother of four and grandmother of half a dozen tend my child, I learned how to relax into motherhood.

Next was Dorothy.

She taught 13-month-old Christopher how to blow a kiss and how to make the sound a dog makes. At Dorothy's, Christopher began to learn the lifelong lesson of getting along. Even though he'll never be the youngest in a family, he experienced the pleasure and pain of just that in Dorothy's house, where she had three older children of her own and neighbor children in and out all day long. Dorothy seemed always to be smiling despite the herd at her feet. Dorothy taught me the joy of children.

After Mary and Dorothy came preschool and the "Misses": Miss Ophelia, Miss Connie, Miss Terri, Miss Eugenia and Miss Jenny.

From these women, Christopher learned the importance of structure and routine. He learned to use his "inside voice" and how to sit in a circle. He learned that tempera is for painting, that rocks sink in water and that you can make a puppet out of a sock.

These women taught my son crafts, songs and skills for life. With their wide knowledge of children, they also fielded the latest concerns of his first-time mother. Whether I was fretting over potty training or a firstborn's tendency toward perfectionism, they always reassured me that my child was as normal as any other. But special. Somehow, they conveyed that my child was average and unique at the same time.

Reciprocal personal relationships with these women continue, years after the professional ones ended.

Dorothy, who once told me that the hardest part about taking care of Christopher was that he wasn't her own, recently sent a card and a crisp $20 bill for Christopher's 5th birthday.

After he opened his gift, Christopher got out his crayons and note paper.

And unprompted, he wrote "I love you" in thanks to the woman who used to carry him around in her arms, even as her own children swarmed around her feet.

This is not a conclusive report about the effects of child care. Nor is it our family's full story. Many's the time I cried, wondering whether I was doing right thing. Many's the time we lost a caregiver and had to go in search of another. One year, we went to four different places before we found the right one.

But for all the negative feelings and talk, for all the guilt that's heaped upon parents for handing their children to "strangers," we sometimes fail to realize what's good about child care.

A dedicated child caregiver, quite literally, cares for—and about—our children.

She shares the burdens and the joys, so much so that when I quit my day job recently and had the opportunity to keep my 5-year-old at home all day,

I decided instead to send him to Miss Trish and Miss Ruth Ann five mornings a week.

This is not to say I believe in shirking parental responsibility. What I believe in is support.

And with community lacking and extended families cities, states and sometimes countries away, we should occasionally feel not guilty, but grateful.

Whether we have to use child care or choose to use it, we should occasionally allow ourselves to feel good that we have people like Ammi Mary, Dorothy and the Misses in our lives.

They are the reason we can call it "child care."

Guilt: Mother knows best

Nov. 5, 1993

A survivor of Catholic schooling, I learned early on that everything is my fault and that I should expect the worst from my mistakes.

Now that I'm a mother, I have perfected that belief, so much so that I wonder if there should be a club for people like me.

"Hi. My name is Mommy, and I'm guilty," the meeting would begin.

"Hi, Mommy," the standing-room-only crowd would shout back.

At a meeting of guilty mothers, a lot of people would show up. Many would report general self-loathing.

"It's all my fault" would be a common refrain, as would "I'm a terrible mother" and "My daughter/son hates me."

Other mothers would be more specific.

"The dentist found two cavities in little Janie's mouth last week," one mom might say, her voice shaking. "I knew I should have kept after her to brush."

Never mind that little Janie is 28 years old. At a meeting of guilty mothers, there would be a lot of talk about the past, about what was done and left undone, also a lot of talk about the future and how our kids are going to turn out because of us.

Never mind that these children also have fathers. We're still the detail people. Suzy develops bronchitis? It's our fault for not curing her common cold. Johnny misbehaves at school? It's because we work outside the home.

There would, of course, be a lot of talk about work.

"I feel guilty because I had to work late last week and made the kids eat takeout two nights in a row."

"I feel guilty because I don't have time to make Halloween costumes like my mother used to."

"Oh, no! Did I miss Halloween again?"

A little guilt in life is good. Guilt makes us act. A mother who slathers a sun-worshipping baby's sensitive skin with Hawaiian Tropic instead of No. 15 undoubtedly will remember next time.

But for many mothers, the constant, modern-day barrage from all sides about what we're supposed to do and not do to keep our kids from being axe murderers, heavy drinkers or bowlegged is too much. It makes us falter. It makes us lose confidence in our ability to make correct choices. It makes us fret and overreact.

At my daughter's 15-month well-baby checkup last month, I beamed when the doctor pronounced my daughter perfect. Except. She should have been off the bottle and on the toothbrush by now. She should be trying to use words instead of still getting what she wants with the grunt-and-point method.

Never mind the three million things I'd done right during the year and a half of my baby's life, I hung my head low for days after that appointment, lifting it mostly to brush the baby's teeth, to thrust a variety of deluxe sippy cups at her and to leave her tired and confused by my sudden verbal assault. "Juice? You want juice? Say juice, honey. That's right, J-U-I-C-E."

My guilty mother's club might provide some relief in instances like these. Instead of languishing alone, saddling our mates with feelings they can't possibly understand, or worse yet, over-correcting or begging for forgiveness from our children, we could wallow with others like ourselves.

For every guilt trip, we could hear about a counter journey.

"I feel guilty for leaving him in time-out too long."

"Why, I feel guilty for not leaving him long enough!"

"I feel guilty for letting him watch 'The Simpsons.' "

"Why, I feel guilty for not letting him watch 'The Simpsons!' "

Guilty. Guilty. Guilty.

Mea culpa. Mea culpa. Mea culpa.

While such a meeting might tend to go on and on, we actually would have no trouble adjourning because eventually somebody would get up and say, "I feel guilty because I'm at this meeting instead of spending time with my children."

And one and all, we would trip on ourselves in our rush to get out the door.

TV-hating Mom stands alone

Nov. 25, 1993

In a living room full of people whose fingers seem poised to turn the on/off button mostly on, I am fighting a losing battle.

My family likes TV. I hate TV. They want to watch TV. I don't want to watch TV. They watch it anyway.

I'm not talking sitcoms here. Thank goodness I'm not talking sitcoms. I'm talking about children who fall out on the floor if they don't see Cookie Monster and Barney six days a week and cartoons on Saturdays. I'm talking about a 5-year-old boy who gets no greater delight than when Mommy's having a bad day. A bad day means the TV will stay on extra long so he and his sister will stay out of Mommy's way.

I'm talking news, in heavy volumes, for my husband, and, of course, sports.

They all watch sports. Off and on throughout the weekend, the TV goes off and on as my husband and his disciples seem determined to witness the weekend's every excellent pitch, touchdown, putt or volley. Even the baby holds her arm up like a triumphant Viking and shouts "Ball!" when she sees it on TV.

Some of this, of course, is worthwhile.

There's some bonding going on between father and child during those quarterback blitzes.

And TV can educate, as is often brought to our attention by our 5-year-old son. The other day, as my husband and I debated the necessity of tuning in the Michigan–Wisconsin game, he walked up to us and said "Cooperation."

Huh?

"Cooperation," he repeated. "People in a family are supposed to work together," he said.

He told us he learned that from Big Bird, who also taught him how to count in Spanish and how cottage cheese and crayons are made.

I like TV like that. Only thing, you can't always find it. I turn on the TV looking to be uplifted, educated and entertained. I am more often horrified, mummified and desensitized—and often without warning.

People tell parents they can protect their kids from bad TV by installing a channel lock. I know different. Christopher's watching a harmless Cubs game with his father, and suddenly, between innings, there's the Terminator blowing up New York with a portable Army tank attached to his arm. During the next break, a woman in a bikini is licking shaving cream off a man's face.

The worst of TV leads me to hate even the best of it, so that about the closest I come to watching TV is when I float in and out of the living room, synthesizing for the kids. Popeye delivers a blow to Bluto, I'm there to smack my lips and say, "Now wouldn't it be better if they solved their problems by talking?"

I make myself particularly available during Saturday morning cartoons so I can explain to Christopher why a good guy like Captain Planet has to use laser beams—or is it numchucks?—to save the environment. I'm also standing by so I can teach him about overconsumption. It's like clockwork: A commercial comes on. Christopher says, "Mommy! I want that!" I say, "Christopher, you can't have everything you want."

I had naively thought when I started a family that I could control this medium—certainly not altogether. I knew when I married my husband that I'd have and hold a certain amount of ESPN. In the trunk of this particular man's car, after all, are golf clubs, a tennis racket, a baseball glove and snow skis—just in case.

I was sure, though, that I could transfer my disdain to my innocents.

Alas, my children are normal. And in our home, TV is power. TV is king. TV is American culture in a magic box, luring my family, like Alice through the Looking Glass.

I find myself sneering at the TV every time I pass by.

It sneers back.

Two's company

April 22, 1994

Should we or shouldn't we?

My husband and I can barely bring ourselves to pose this question to each other, and so we ask strangers like Bev and Bob, a bug-eyed couple we met at a birthday party with their 5-year-old son, 2-year-old daughter and a hip-held baby of indecipherable age and gender.

They didn't even pretend.

"Don't do it," they said.

Three kids upsets the balance, they said. Three means one child feels left out. Three kids sends parents over the edge.

Indeed, we're hard-pressed to find a single, sound reason why we should have a third child. This is unlike a first child, which you have for reasons that are too many to count. As for the second, you want the first to have a playmate. Or you want to try for the other gender.

What with overstretched families the status quo, not to mention $20,000-

a-year college educations, three is a little harder to announce to people like your mother, who has been listening to you complain about two.

"Haven't you figured out what causes that by now?" I can hear mine snapping.

Both my mother and my husband's mother had four kids. Four was a normal number during their era of child-rearing. But a generation later, you'd think three kids was three dozen, with few people taking the plunge past a pair. Today's American woman has an average 2.1 children, down even from 20 years ago when the average was 2.5.

People who study family say the continued downward trend that started in the 1960s is partly due to both parents working and being overstretched on time and money. Families don't need all those kids to work the farm anymore anyway. It's also believed to be due to a deeper understanding of children. An increasing number of parents are learning that children deserve to be valued. Many parents today, busier than ever, believe they can give greater quality to smaller numbers.

At two and two, our family feels manageable. Two boys. Two girls. Two parents. Two children. On long car rides, my husband entertains one while I watch for cows with the other. When our two children grow up, assuming they are speaking to us and each other, we could have a tidy foursome for cards.

The intelligent choice would be to stop at two, particularly considering my age and energy level, not to mention the overpopulation of the world. There's also ear infections to consider. Our kids' medical charts, which include the documentation of hundreds of phone calls and office visits and 5.5 sets of corrective ear tubes which have yet to correct, could be made into a movie. A third child could send me to the brink if I caught him tugging at his ear.

But how do you stop at the intelligent part when the emotions are so strong? How do you stop having babies once you start?

I shake my head in wonder when I see a woman in the grocery store with more little children than hands, one clinging to one hand, one in her arms, a third stepping on her toes.

I also marvel at my baby daughter, at her soft skin, her pure white teeth. Her dimples and her saucer eyes. The way the sun shines straight through her hair when the wind picks it up in back, how determined she is to walk, talk and grow.

I can't imagine never doing this again. I can't imagine giving up the process, the pregnancy, the labor and the birth. The child.

I just got started.

I tell myself that despite the reports of exhaustion we hear from parents with multiple children, plenty of people have larger families today and thrive.

Maybe my husband and I are masochists. It is odd that we're thinking about upsetting the equilibrium right about the time our existing two children started playing together, right about the time I squeezed into my favorite jeans again.

Or maybe we're optimists. Maybe we like bearing and raising children. Maybe we think by continuing to have children, we continue to demonstrate a love of life and a hope for the future of our world.

Maybe we think we can make it work like we have everything else. And then we'll be left with one truly scary thought: Where there are three, could an even four be far behind?

Christmas magic

Dec. 19, 1993

When I was a little girl, Christmas was simple. All I had to do was get up and go see what Santa brought me.

Later, as a single adult, I tried to keep it uncomplicated. I made Christmas by putting candles in the windows, "White Christmas" on the stereo and cinnamon sticks in a simmering pot on the stove. Those were the days when I could stay awake for midnight mass.

Then I became a wife and mother.

And like my mother before me, who one year stitched 25 Barbie outfits for me and my sister, I went from sending a few Christmas cards to addressing, personalizing, and sometimes making 150 of them.

I went from buying a few Christmas decorations and presents to making my own wrapping paper and door hangings, cookies and presents for relatives and friends.

I went from saying "Merry Christmas" to the neighbors in passing to standing over the stove making dozens of pecan pralines to give to them.

Every year, I think about going back to the simpler kind of Christmas. I even bought *Unplug the Christmas Machine* by Jean Coppock Staehili and Jo Robinson a few years back. It's a charming book, which tells us how we can put more love and warmth in the season by focusing more on family togetherness, peace and the spirit of Christmas. Inside the book is an entire chapter devoted to "Women: The Christmas Magicians," which suggests ways for us to give up some of our holiday activities.

Every year around Thanksgiving, I bring the book down from the shelf. Then I put it aside and start the frenzy all over again.

My husband doesn't understand this. He hears me yelling at the pralines because they won't coagulate and at my first Christmas sweatshirt because I used glitter paint instead of regular. He sees me falling into bed at night. He reminds me that nobody's making me to do all this.

But after a few years I think I'm beginning to understand why I do anyway.

We magicians might experience a lot of fatigue and stress at Christmas. We also experience the magic.

As a child, someone gave the magic to me. Now I have children. I want them to experience as full and beautiful a Christmas as was given to me.

But it's more than even that.

Every time I experience something of Christmas, I go back, to a wondrous time when I was a little girl peeking around the corner of the darkened living room on Christmas morning.

Those pecan pralines? For as long as I can remember pralines were waiting for me under my grandmother's tree. I taste my own pralines and I am playing under her Christmas tree with my cousins.

Sitting in the floor curling ribbon for gifts takes me back to a Christmas a long time ago when my mother taught me how to hold onto one blade of the scissors and pull.

Many's the time during the Christmas season when I find myself yelling at a driver in the shopping mall parking lot, gritting my teeth, agonizing over some detail, like whether my son is old enough this year to sit through "The Nutcracker."

But many more's the time when I find myself tingling with excitement, cheered and warmed, like I've just drunk a mug of spiced cider.

I do it for my family. My family includes me. 'Tis the season to remember.

Finding common ground

Jan. 27, 1994

Partly because they live more than 1,000 miles apart, the six children of my husband and his siblings had been brought together only once before, during a short visit three years ago.

Yet when they were finally reunited during the recent winter holiday, the six young cousins raced to each other with an uncanny sense of family.

Each hardly knew what the other looked like. And yet the cousins immediately attached themselves to each other, insisting even that first night that they sleep together in the same room of my husband's brother's house. For a week, they hardly knew their parents existed but found ways to absorb all there was of each other.

My husband and I have often worried that our children won't have the same understanding of family that we had growing up.

Like my husband, I grew up living in the same town with almost all my extended family, including two sets of grandparents and one set of great grandparents.

Every holiday, if not after church on Sundays, various and huge collections of family gathered, including aunts and uncles, grandparents and great-grandparents and cousins–first cousins, second cousins, cousins once removed, twice removed, and every other kind there is. I can to this day conjure the smell of each grandmother's house and how I felt when my best-looking boy cousin grinned at me.

My son and daughter don't come close to that kind of existence.

These days, most of my side of the family lives 600 miles away in one direction. Most of my husband's family lives 1,000 miles in the other. One of his sisters lives a seven-day drive from us.

We try to keep in touch by phone, holding the receiver to the children's ears so they'll know the voice of Uncle Jim and Aunt Sharon. We visit some family members once a year or so. Others we see much less often.

We wish that we could give our children what we had growing up. We worry that they won't understand the meaning of family outside Mom and Dad.

And yet, during our holiday visit, our children showed us that they know.

The baby, who's at an age when nobody but Mommy will do, somehow knew it was OK to go to the outstretched arms of her Aunt Cappy the third day she knew her. With little squabbling, we were able to leave both children with their grandmother overnight on New Year's Eve.

Our son and daughter showed us most especially in their relationships with the other young people, their cousins, mutual innocents who stretch out their arms without even knowing they are.

Even as the adults struggled after all these years to find common ground in such safe and emotionless topics as money and weather, the children played and fought, tattled and forgave and snuggled in each other's arms.

I hope always to remember the Christmas Eve service we attended. All the cousins, dressed in turtlenecks and Christmas sweaters against the lightly falling snow outside, sat side by side in the dimly lit cathedral. All except my son. My 5-year-old son, who thinks everybody in the world has cooties, suddenly climbed into the lap of his oldest cousin and laid his head on her shoulder. The two of them sat listening with rapt attention to the children's choir, unaware that I couldn't take my eyes off the sameness, the surety, the sense of belonging, pure and solid and joyful, that I saw.

We came away with good news from this trip. Our children hold family in their hearts, despite the distance.

My husband and I also came away knowing that we have to do this more often. Not just for the children's furthered understanding, not just for their memory banks.

But for ours, for my husband and his siblings, who once shared much, who now think they have to search for common ground.

They know now that the next time they get together, they'll only have to go as far as my brother-in-law's upstairs bedroom on the right. There, they'll find their common ground, sleeping in tiny sleeping bags on the floor, bodies and hearts entangled, pure and solid and joyful.

Judge not...

Feb. 10, 1994

Once you become a parent, you become fair game to any number of family, friends and strangers who are certain they can parent your children much better than you.

Take whining. (Please.)

As in most homes with young children, the frequency with which my husband and I hear the pitter-patter of little feet is second only to the frequency with which we withstand the frustrated communication efforts of our nonverbal baby daughter.

Likewise, her brother. He knows how to talk. But he has reverted recently to shrieking, grunting and moaning because he sees his sister getting all the attention that way.

All kinds of armchair experts, including my mother, who cares about my mental health, tell me to ignore it, and it'll go away.

With all due respect to people who mean well, and OK, my mother, can a dog ignore a dog whistle? Or a teacher, nails screeching on a chalkboard? Can a firefighter tune out a fire alarm?

I'd like to know when's the last time some of these advisers spent a month sequestered with a young child. Are they parents themselves?

In fact, many haven't a clue what it's like to feed, clothe, and chase a child several times a day for several years so that every now and then you slip and/or learn the hard way.

And yet every time my family and I are in the company of this particular newlywed couple I know, they inevitably will look at our imperfect children and say, "OUR children will NEVER misbehave."

I can't wait for this couple to breed so I can meet children who keep still, quiet and clean on demand.

Of course, it's not just people without kids. People with kids having ONE perfect day are great at LOOKING like they have all the answers. Especially when you don't.

I got a look in a bookstore the other day, where I admit we shouldn't have been, since it was one of those days when the kids were whining in unison but not in harmony, and I was in the fever pitch of PMS, which does, by the way, exist.

As soon as we entered the library-like atmosphere, both kids, delirious to get away from me, hit the floor running and screaming, piercing the quiet weekday afternoon. Snarling and growling like a mad bear, I stormed after the one who has the greater potential to destroy. Before I could get to her, she grabbed the most expensive magazine in the store and loudly ripped off its cover.

As if being horrified at the behavior of myself and my children weren't enough, I had to stumble over Gandhi sitting crosslegged on the floor and reading quietly to the two perfect angels in his lap.

His brow furrowing contemptuously, Mr. Peaceful Countenance actually stopped reading just so he could stare up at me with a look that said, "I'm a perfect parent. And you're not."

Like he's never had a bad day.

We should take a vow when we become parents that we won't judge each other: not a woman snapping at her children in the checkout line, not a post-menopausal woman who decides to have a baby, or a mother who feeds her children cereal for supper. We can't possibly know what sends one woman over the edge and what makes another want a brand-new baby at 59. And cereal is fortified.

There are all kinds of ways to be good parents. Some of us remember to take moist towelettes and bibs to the restaurant when we go out to eat with the kids.

Others, like me, forget to remind the kids to wash up at home and frequently find they've drawn all over their hand-me-downs at the end of the day.

But I also taught those hands to play pat-a-cake. And I hug and kiss what's in those clothes a lot.

All of us good parents have good days. All of us have bad. All of us have our own tolerance levels, our own ways and means of doing things, our own rhythms that only we—and maybe our children—understand and become accustomed to. I think we should respect our own rhythms. Others should, too.

A friend of mine, a psychologist, often counsels clients who are parents. She tells them that it's more important that we trust ourselves, rather than what others have to say.

"Each of us raises the kind of child we can live with," she tells them.

Does that mean mine will never stop whining?

Mothers and their sons

Feb. 24, 1994

We have so far managed to avoid buying our son a cap gun, camouflage clothes or anything having to do with G.I. Joe.

This doesn't mean our red-blooded American boy doesn't defend against the enemy.

A plastic clothes hanger easily stretches in his hands to become a bow for an invisible arrow. A yardstick becomes a sword. A Y-shaped stick and a rubber band is a slingshot. A gang of boys, an Army unit.

"Christopher!" I shouted incredulously the first time I saw him surrounded by a platoon of neighborhood boys holding various homemade weapons.

The boys stopped and stared, perplexed as to why Christopher's mother was calling him inside.

To this Woodstock-era mother, who taught her young son to hug teddy bears and to pet the cat gently—and who didn't have any brothers to teach her about boys—this kind of activity is bad.

To them, it's child's play.

What's more, a lot of peace-loving children's advocates, including Mr. Rogers, believe it's important child's play.

These same advocates readily acknowledge that some children, particularly those exposed to too much real violence, might be at risk for war play if they don't know where play ends and the real world begins.

But Fred Rogers and others say that as long as children have other interests, as long as they aren't hurting each other, as long as they don't transfer this brand of conflict resolution to the real world, war play can be healthy. War and superhero play help children work out their feelings about the very violence they fear. War play gives children power when they normally have none.

It's a strange world we live in if violence can actually be good. And yet it stands to reason that kids need to play out the harsh realities of the real world. Besides, what choice do I have?

Even if I could stop him from systematically laying traps for Catwoman, my son would still say "Ay-yah!" and karate-kick the air several hundred times a day. This is what boys do. This is what girls would do, too, given half a chance to explore all their feelings and interests, say Nancy Carlsson-Paige and Diane E. Levin, co-authors of *Who's Calling the Shots: How to Respond Effectively to Children's Fascination With War Play and War Toys.*

This doesn't mean I like watching my son go "Pow-Pow!" with Tinkertoys or that I've surrendered my nonviolent position. I will continue monitoring my son's violent play to make sure the violence is appropriate, if there's such a thing.

I will still say "No" to storebought weapons, which look so real these days they make my spine crawl, which is where children's advocates bail out, too; it's one thing to pick up a stick in the backyard and make up a game. It's another to use glitzy toys that glorify killing. So far, since all the other parents on the block are likewise avoiding the latest Super Soaker at Toys R Us, I'm winning this particular battle.

But I'm afraid this controlled innocence won't last forever.

I thought I had it bad when I caught him and his friends shooting each other with sticks.

There more than likely will come a time when my son's contact peers will not only include boys with whole armies in their toy boxes, but boys who get their kicks by putting homemade bombs in mailboxes, shooting birds with BB guns, or worse, these days.

I can only wonder how many more compromises I'll make as I reassure myself, "Boys will be boys."

Tell me a story, Mommy

March 10, 1994

Whenever he's bored or he can't get to sleep, or maybe he just wants to be close, my 5-year-old son asks me for stories of a particular ilk.

"Tell me about when you were a little girl, Mommy," he says sleepily.

My son wants to know all there is to know about growing up in the "white house," as he calls the childhood home that I've taken him to many times.

It is a time that I now know was difficult, living as I did with parents who were too young and too incompatible to have gotten married, much less have four children. There was never enough money, never enough commitment. And in the end, when I was 14 and just beginning to blossom, and my sisters were 7, 9 and 15, there was a divisive and bitter divorce that has haunted me into my adulthood.

But for my son, I easily, only, recall the sweetness and light of childhood, which, to his delight, I can't stop relating once I get started.

"Uh-huh," he says, his eyelids beginning to droop.

He's asleep. And I'm still remembering the excitement of summer approaching and asking my mother every day after school, "Mama, is it warm enough?" "No, not today," she would answer for an endless number of days until, finally: "Yes, you can wear your new red flip-flops. And you can play under the sprinkler, too."

For my son, I'm on the back porch, helping my mother watch the ice cream churn, which is filled with berries just picked in the woods behind our house. I'm lying with my head in her lap while she cleans my ears. She's tucking me in to her bed to watch a day of "Andy Griffith" and "Leave it To Beaver" because I'm sick. She's leading my Girl Scout meeting, taking us to the Y and basketball and Olan Mills and making sure I get to join the junior high sorority even though we can't afford it. She is strong and so beautiful.

I'm seeing the many things my father could do with his hands, from planting peaches, cucumbers and shrubbery in the backyard, to building on to houses and repairing our toys. I'm feeling the wind float through the pines as I sit high up in the tree house that he built, removed from whichever sister is bothering me at the moment. I am in the backseat of the big, white station wagon that my father is driving for our weekly Sunday outing to the mountains. I am feeling proud that he has laughed at something I've said.

I am remembering family dinners every night around the oval kitchen table and birthday parties with relatives in the backyard. I am remembering a family trip one summer to the Georgia beaches and to Washington, D.C., all in the same week. My parents are in the front of the station wagon. And I am in the back again, in my pajamas with my sisters, safe and warm. Happy.

For my son, I remember that my parents tried.

I know now that they also struggled. For a while in my early adult years as I began to look back, the struggle was all I could remember.

Now, as a mother passing along history to her son, the good stories are the ones I remember most while the pain fades into unimportance.

In the 1993 book, *Sacred Stories: A Celebration of the Power of Stories to Transform and Heal*, writer Sam Keen talks about the importance of storytelling. By telling our stories to our children, we provide them with continuity and a guiding set of principles, Keen says.

By telling our stories out loud over and over, we discover and rediscover ourselves. We find a new reality. We find healing. Things that once seemed so big, put in the proper context and perspective, sometimes aren't so big anymore.

As he was settling in the other night, Christopher wanted more stories, this time about Easter Sunday in our family.

And so I told stories about overflowing baskets covered in colored cellophane, about Easter dresses that my mother sewed and family dinners at my paternal grandmother's house, about egg dyes and egg hunts and the cake my mother made every year to look like a basket with green coconut on top for grass.

Christopher and I also talked about the Easter season three years ago when he was 2 and we visited the house where my father lived with his second wife.

His brow furrowing with the sudden realization, Christopher asked the question I'd always braced myself for: "But Mommy, why did Poppy not always live with Grandma?"

I took a deep breath. And then I told him people sometimes decide they don't want to be married anymore. He wanted to know if that means they take off their rings.

Then he fell asleep.

The secret was out. It didn't sound nearly so bad, anymore.

And so I kissed him and went to bed, while visions of Easter baskets, of family and togetherness, of the good times, prevailed in my head.

Love isn't all you need, after all

April 7, 1994

I remember when I was pregnant with our first child telling my husband it didn't matter whether we had enough money, parenting skills or good schools in the neighborhood.

Like the Beatles, I was convinced that love is all you need.

And sure enough, in the beginning, everything was beautiful simply because we adored this little person who brought teddy bear wallpaper and the sweet smell of baby powder to our spare bedroom.

But babies turn into children.

And one day, listening to my 18-month-old scream because he wanted something he couldn't have, it dawned on me that children might need a few other things to survive and thrive, like discipline.

I still remember how proud I felt the first time he responded to a disciplinary technique.

"Christopher," I had said, "I want you to get in the car seat by the time I count to three."

I was also relieved. I had no idea what I would do if he hadn't obediently climbed into his seat.

But respond he did. And so love and discipline became my prescription for raising a child.

And then my son marched off to preschool. And the job of parent became slightly more complicated, what with classmates acting like Ninja Turtles and teachers doling out their own combination of academics and learning through play.

I realized then how important it is to be aware of what my child is doing when I'm not there so that I can act accordingly when I am. If I know he's had gooey Rice Krispie treats for snack at school, for example, I can easily ban sugar for the rest of the day.

And so I added "parental involvement" to love and discipline. And my list kept growing.

I learned the hard way, after my second child got into a bottle of medicine, that my children can't possibly know not to chase the pretty ball into the street unless I teach them. And so I added "safekeeper" and "protector of health" to my list.

I added "undivided time" when I realized how impossible it is to really sink your teeth into what your children are saying and doing while you're washing the dishes, running out the door or sitting on the other side of the bathroom door.

And soon enough, I began to realize that the description of the hardest job I'll ever do is open-ended, ever-changing and increasingly complicated.

From my humble beginnings as a flower child who dreamed of keeping her baby alive with her love, I learned that love is only the beginning.

It is a good beginning. Psychologists say even a child who has experienced the most difficult of childhoods probably will thrive if he was loved by someone.

Love is my favorite part. Love doesn't require any pre-planning or money. Love makes me do things with my kids not because I should, but just because.

I love lifting them to touch the ceiling because I know it makes them feel tall. I love sitting close and reading books after baths at night because their soft, clean skin feels so nice next to mine. Nothing is more beautiful to me than when I tell my 21-month-old daughter that I love her and she takes her thumb out of her mouth long enough to say "Yuh you" back.

Unfortunately, I know now, love is not the only requirement for being a parent. It is simply the easy part. And the propellant. It is what motivates me to provide them with boundaries and rules, rides to soccer practice and birthday parties, to instill values and set good examples, to keep one ear cocked at all times.

It is naive, I now believe, to think that love is all you need. But I don't think I was that far off the mark. I would amend the Beatles' song only slightly. Love is all you need to begin.

No more baby steps

June 30, 1994

Their eyes were big. Their tiny, tasseled caps were teetering on their little heads. It was time for the graduating class of 35 students to process into the church as only this graduating class could.

One girl closed her eyes. Another giggled and broke into a run. A dimple-faced boy stuffed his hands inside the pockets of his khaki shorts and beamed with pride. A diminutive girl with doe eyes yelled "Stop it!" when the audience began to chuckle because she was so cute.

During the ceremony, colorful diplomas decorated with pictures of children and certifying students as having completed the "preschool course of study," were distributed. White carnations were presented to mothers who looked for all the world as if they were the ones being honored. The preschool director told the children she hoped they remembered to love each other, and the class sang a song their teacher taught them about the importance of family and friends.

Later in the reception hall there was white cake and red punch, and pictures were snapped of friends with their arms slung across each other's shoulders. The Most Frequently Posed must have been a little girl named Veronica who throughout the year was also The Most Kissed by Boys.

There were gifts given to beloved teachers who had doubled as mothers and who now posed, too, their eyes brimming as little boys jumped in their arms and buried their heads in their shoulders to say good-bye.

There was talk about why preschool graduation always means there's hardly a dry eye behind the camcorders and 35mms.

"Things will go fast from here," my son's teacher said.

Whether the kids knew the significance of the occasion was hard to tell, although it's certain they knew something was up. Our son had trouble sleeping for a week before Graduation Day.

"Is kindergarten hard, Mommy?" he wanted to know.

We told him no, that he will do just fine.

Only we know how things will change.

No more play school after this. No more going to school just because. No more leaving for two weeks in the middle of the year because we want to go on vacation.

Next year, the 4-year-olds will all have turned 5, which means they will leave home every morning because it's required. Their teachers will teach them certain lessons not because it's fun but because the entry requirements for first grade are pressing on them. And then second grade. And third and fourth. And so it will be forevermore: reading and writing, listening and sitting still, pressure and projects, homework and progress reports. Beginning next year, kids will be held back or pushed on. There will be dashed hopes and greater expectations.

For our son and his parents, there will be an even greater adjustment. What with the state of the economy forcing employers to offer temporary jobs instead of permanent ones, we are preparing to move to another state for the second time this year. We don't know yet whether my husband's new job will extend beyond next summer or what our new house will look like, much less which school Christopher will attend. We tell him kindergarten won't be hard. We don't tell him life won't be.

It seems overly attentive, all this attention given to one tiny passage of life in the lives of ones so young. There will be many more graduation caps, many more times that "Pomp and Circumstance" will make the mothers cry and the fathers brace themselves so they won't. But barring potty training, this is the first real milepost.

I took two dozen pictures and I kept going back for one more.

The teacher told me Christopher probably won't remember this day when I pull out the photos even a few years from now.

But I will. I'll remember the Graduation Day when his hair was so shiny and soft that his little red cap wouldn't stay on, when his pin-striped Oxford cloth shirt was stained by red punch and white cake, when his life and my heart were full of only hope and promise.

About the author

Journalist Debra-Lynn B. Hook, 39, has been chronicling life with children in her "Bringing Up Mommy" newspaper column since she was pregnant with her first child. Today, she is the mother of Christopher, 6, and Emily, 2½, and her popular biweekly column has appeared in *Reader's Digest, The Chicago Tribune, The Atlanta Constitution, San Jose Mercury News, St. Paul Pioneer Press, The Kansas City Star, The Wichita Eagle-Beacon, The Lexington Herald-Leader, The Albuquerque Journal, The Montreal Gazette* and numerous other newspapers. Debra-Lynn, who spent her youth in the Carolinas and Louisiana, lives today in Columbia, Mo., with her children and her husband, Steve, a political scientist at the University of Missouri. A full-time newspaper reporter for 12 years, Debra-Lynn left that job two years ago to spend more time with her children and to continue her career as a writer and consultant with an emphasis on family. This is her first book.